Life, Lyrics & Lockdown

Life, Lyrics & Lockdown

Finding peace in changing circumstances

Gloria Kearney

www.ambassador-international.com

LIFE, LYRICS AND LOCKDOWN

Illustrations by Lynsey Grierson

Paperback: ISBN:978-1-64960-191-9
eBook: eISBN:978-1-64960-197-1

Printed in UK

Ambassador International

Emerald House
411 University Ridge, Suite B14
Greenville, SC 29601
www.ambassador-international.com

Ambassador Books and Media
The Mount
2 Woodstock Link
Belfast, BT6 8DD, Northern Ireland, UK
www.ambassadormedia.co.uk

Contents

Preface

For the past six years, I have been referring to 'Songs from a Quiet Heart' as my 'final' book but Lockdown in 2020 has changed all that. During the first ten weeks of this strange, surreal period in all of our lives, I often woke up in the early morning with lines of poetry running through my mind, a poem for each week! Some folks who read them encouraged me to think of publishing them but I knew that a book needed more content than ten poems and a wider focus than Lockdown. So I decided to place them in the context of the past five years - years of changing circumstances in our lives.

The belief that it was something God was calling me to do came during a Zoom meeting with my church family - three prophetic words were given to me by Azman, Tucker and Zoe:

'God is going to ignite something new in you.'

'Gloria, I'm not sure about this but is there a book happening?'

'I see your head set in the frame of the painting behind you' (that spoke to me of the framework or structure that is needed when writing a book.)

When the first email I read the next morning included the words 'maybe by the end of lockdown you'll have a new book', I decided that maybe God was trying to say something to me!

I began writing and collating the next day and such was the compulsion I felt (often rising early to work on it) that the initial draft was completed in three weeks - something of a miracle for me, as previous books have taken a year or even two years to write!

I'm grateful...

to Robert and Ellie (our granddaughter from Australia, who has been living with us since January) for giving me the space to concentrate on writing - apologies for the scrappy meals! I'll make it up to you... maybe!

to Niall, who proofread the first draft, for your eagle eyes - hope all the missing commas and hyphens are in!

to Lynsey, for the wonderful illustrations - you're a talented friend

to Richard for agreeing to write the foreword - your thoughtful consideration of the text and your kind words are greatly appreciated

to John and Claire from Journey Community Church, for your contributions - so glad I was able to include your stories

to Crawford from Ballynahinch Baptist Church and Ali from Grace Fellowship for reading the manuscript and encouraging me to publish it

to RT Kendall, Philip Yancey, Don McMinn and the Ancient Hebrew Research Centre for allowing me to include quotes from your books

to Pat, Gwen and Lavinia, my prayer partners of many years and the OliveTree prayer group in Journey Community Church - your enthusiasm for the project and your prayer support were a great encouragement

to Emma and Willow, my granddaughters, for inspiring one of the poems and allowing me to include the great photograph you took

to the granddaughters I haven't mentioned yet - Freya, Charlotte and Cora - for being fabulous granddaughters!

to the rest of my crazy, far-flung family - for all the fun we have when we get together

to Mark and the folks at Ambassador, for agreeing to publish yet another book - thanks for all you have done

to the Unchanging One who has enabled me to find peace in changing circumstances - my heart is full of praise for Your unfailing love and Your grace which is always sufficient.

FOREWORD

Life, Lyrics and Lockdown caught me by surprise. As I read through the pages, I found myself smiling. At times in my most humbling humbleness, I thought:

'I wish I said that.'

'Why didn't I think of that?'

'That would make a great sermon.'

As humans, we want to own. We want to control. We often want more. We can't help it. The path this leads us down is bothersome. Some end up in a dark cave, others leap out and embrace the goodness of life. This book is for those who want to leap.

We grab and acquire; Jesus says, 'No, give it away.'

We want to be in charge; Jesus says, 'No, come follow me.'

We reach beyond our grasp and Jesus says, 'Yes! Yes! Yes! Keep stretching.'

'Blessed are those who hunger and thirst for righteousness, for they will be filled.'

This book is for those who attend church every Sunday and walk away thinking, 'There must be more than this.'

The narrative you hold in your hand is a pilgrimage about a pilgrimage. It is honest, real and authentic. It's like sitting down to a spiritual meal, wiping our mouth and then asking for another helping. Spiritual hunger breeds spiritual thirst. Thirst draws us out of our caves, our comfort and security. Then we brashly hold up our cup and ask for the overflow.

Life: Gloria marches through the pages describing her spiritual journey. It's taken her to a place many of us want to go, but are not sure how to get there. The confessions and insights are stepping stones leading us to the sea. The challenge is to take the plunge and watch God part the waters we couldn't navigate alone.

Lyrics: This book is more than a story. Like the Psalms of David, Gloria's poetry is dynamic and relative to the journey she's leading us on. They are emotive. They're the heartbeat of the text.

Lockdown: A virus has forced the world into a cave. I don't believe anyone is at peace with the new world order. For many, it's a wilderness. We watch the world change before our eyes and wonder where we are heading. Luke, however, tells us Jesus went into the wilderness 'full of the Holy Spirit' but he came out in the 'power of the Holy Spirit'. We all want to come out of this better, not worse. This book is an inspiration and comfort to all of us who want to walk in God's new order and not the one the world is thrusting on us.

Finding peace in changing circumstances: No one is a stranger to change. Some changes we desire, others are forced upon us but we don't have to crumble under any of them. However, we all need a helping hand now and then to pass on through. In these pages, Gloria is reaching out that friendly hand. It's not just her story, but it is a story of the God who watches our back and comforts and leads us in our time of need - especially when the walls seem to be closing in around us.

This is a little book with a big heart. The challenge is to keep leaping, keep reaching, keep trusting and don't forget the Christian God we follow is the winner and he's taking us with him to the finish line. Thank you, Gloria. The story is a good one!

Rev. Richard Porter

Retired Pastor And Old Testament lecturer: Church of the Nazarene
Pastor Emeritus, Journey Community Church
Author, The Kingdom of God - The Director's Cut (release date, June 2021)

CHAPTER 1

CHANGE

Life can change in a moment! I was busy working in my kitchen a few years ago (2017 to be precise) when one of my prayer partners rang.

'Did you know there's a group who meet in the St Patrick's Centre to pray for Downpatrick?' asked Lavinia. 'I'd like to go - would you be interested in coming with me?'

I knew immediately that this was a significant moment as I experienced a physical resonance deep inside - almost as though I'd been very gently punched in my stomach - an unusual response to an invitation to a prayer meeting! Little did I know that, as a result of this moment, life would never be the same again. That prayer meeting marked the beginning of our journey into Journey - a community church that would eventually be planted in Downpatrick.

At that time, Robert and I had been members of the Baptist Church in Ballynahinch for 35 years - a church we loved dearly, where we had been honoured to serve in various ways. Some of our closest friends attended the church, including my 3 prayer partners, Lavinia, Pat and Gwen. We had been praying together, laughing together and crying together for many years. We had supported each other in our ministries and our miseries - as Lavinia informed us one day,

'God likes to turn misery into ministry!'

My heart had been for Ballynahinch through all those 35 years - I had taught in one of its schools, had joined in Churches

Together services and a Churches Together prayer meeting, I had prayer walked its streets and sung carols in its square and around its estates at Christmas time. I was happy, content and busy. But change was on the heart of God and He began to prepare my heart to receive it.

My desire to hear God's voice had long been deep inside but I found it growing and increasing as I began to take time out on quiet days to be still before Him and listen for His whisper in my heart. I asked for prayer for discernment and expressed my desire, as I often do, by writing a poem, inspired by the question Jesus asked the blind man in Mark 10:

"'What do you want me to do for you?' Jesus asked.

'My Rabbi', the blind man said, 'I want to see!"

DISCERNMENT

What would you have me do?
The Master said to me.
My answer came from deep within,
I want, O Lord, to see.

To have the veil pulled back, my Lord,
To see, discern, to know,
Be sure just how and when to speak
Which prayers to pray, which way to go.

I want to have discernment, Lord,
To sense the enemy's hand,
Be quick to see the schemes he has
Against my life, my church, my land.

I want to walk in truth, O Lord,
Be Spirit- filled and led,
Step into all Your plans for me,
And by Your Word be fed.

I want to see as You saw, Lord,
Those sad, oppressed and lost,
I want to minister Your grace,
Refuse to count the cost.

So at Your feet I bow,
Reach out Your hand to me,
Remove the veil that clouds my sight,
I want, O Lord, to see.

2014

I knew that I didn't always see people as Jesus saw them - others saw a blind man but Jesus saw a disciple who could see; in Matthew, others saw a greedy tax collector but Jesus saw a church leader and a Gospel writer; others saw a sinful woman at Sychar's well but Jesus saw an evangelist; others looked at John and Mary standing at the cross and saw two mourners but Jesus saw a new family. If I wanted to minister His grace, I needed to discover a new way of seeing.

Even as I wrote the poem, I knew that I was also being challenged by the too numerous times that God wanted me to see with His eyes, but I didn't want to look! I could sing the little chorus 'To be like Jesus' with feeling and fervour but the realisation that I was far from sharing His compassion for the sad, oppressed and lost would lead me, sometime later, to write a prayer of repentance:

'It all starts with seeing, being willing to open my eyes to the hurt and pain all around me. Forgive me, Lord, too often I walk through life with blinkers on, seeing only what concerns me, having a narrow, restricted view. I sort through the post and throw away the appeal letters, afraid that if I open them, my heart might be touched by the sad face with the tear on the cheek. I walk into the shop and try to ignore the Big Issue seller who sits there so patiently, day after day, in the cold and the rain. I switch off the news after the headlines, afraid that if I see the suffering caused by war or disease, then my heart might break.

But if I want to be like Jesus... I have to see as He saw. So help me take the blinkers off.

Compassion comes next... a deep, heartfelt sorrow at what I've seen. Needy people don't always come at a convenient time! The crowd came to Jesus at a time of grief and pain, but He didn't turn them away... He had compassion. I need to know more of Your compassion, Lord... that willingness to put myself out for someone, to change my schedule to suit theirs, to spend time listening to their stories. Sometimes needy people aren't easy to see, they don't always shout for attention, so I need You to give me a greater sensitivity to those around me.

If I want to be like Jesus... I have to feel as He felt. Soften this heart of mine, Lord.

The seeing and the feeling have to lead to action - true compassion will always lead to action. This is where I'm weakest, Lord, sometimes using the excuse that I'm busy to avoid taking action. Jesus gave His time and energy so generously and so consistently to the people around Him, to His community. He ministered to their needs, teaching and healing even at times of pressure and difficulty for Himself. Ultimately His compassion led to a cross.

And I want to be like Jesus... I have to do as He did. What if it leads to an even busier life? What if it leads me outside my comfort zone? What if it leads to self-sacrifice? What if it leads to a cross?'

To begin with, it just led to a change of church...

CHAPTER 2

PEACE IN CHANGE

We don't always handle change well. We feel uncomfortable when the ground beneath us begins to shift when the familiar becomes unfamiliar, the stable becomes unstable and the certainty of knowing is lost. Unfortunately, life rarely remains the same - change always seems to be just around the corner. It's good to remember that God can see around the corner and often works in us to prepare our hearts for the big changes up ahead.

When I look back at the notes I made for meetings I was invited to speak at during the period leading up to our change of church, I can see how God was preparing my own heart even as I prepared my talks for others. For many months, a recurring theme was Peace. Verses such as John 14:27 became the starting point for various talks:

> *'I am leaving you with a gift - peace of mind and heart. And the peace I give is a gift the world cannot give. So don't be troubled or afraid.'* (NLT)

I researched the meaning of the word 'peace' (Shalom in Hebrew) and discovered a rich breadth I hadn't realised before:

'completeness, wholeness, health, peace, welfare, safety, tranquillity, prosperity, perfectness, fullness, harmony, absence of agitation or discord'.

When a Jew used the greeting 'Shalom', he was saying 'Peace to you - I hope you have all the highest good coming your way.'

Some Native American translations struck a chord too:

'To sit down in one's heart', 'a quiet heart' and 'quiet goodness'.

What a rich seam of truth! I could be sure of God's Shalom in my own life.

Being asked to speak on the seasons of life helped me to realise that every season has its challenges and anxieties but our God can change an anxious heart into a quiet heart if we just lean into Him in the tough times. Paul wrote about finding contentment in every circumstance:

> *'I can do everything through Christ who gives me strength.'* (Philippians 4:12) NLT

I could have peace, whatever!

PEACE WHATEVER

The storms of life rage all around
Fierce winds of trouble never cease
Time after time they buffet me
But still, my heart's at peace.

Deep sorrow visits every door
Bearing her gifts of tears and pain
But when she knocks, the Master's voice
Promises peace again.

The closest friend can wield a sword
Destroy a friendship, wish me ill
But even as I reel from hurt
I hear His voice say, 'Peace, be still'.

So, far below the surface pain
Life's clamour and its din
My heart is quietly assured
His peace reigns deep within.

2014

Psalm 139 underlined the concept of 'Whatever' and became the basis of other talks -

Whatever I do or say, my sitting, rising, thinking, going out, coming in, speaking - in all the stuff of life, I am known, embraced and encircled in His Love.

Whatever place I am in, the heavens, the depths, the far side of the sea, I am guided and held fast.

Whatever situation I face, whatever wrong thing I have done, whatever the enemy throws at me, I do not need to fear for He is still with me.

God reminded me often that His peace is found in His Presence. On one occasion, during our usual Friday prayer time, God silenced all four of us and for a long time, we simply stayed in His Presence, awestruck.

AWESTRUCK

Before Your splendour, I'm in awe,
Before Your majesty I bow,
Oh how I long to catch
A glimpse of Glory now.

My spirit struggles to express
My praise in thought or word,
Pull back the veil that hides Your face,
Reveal Your glory, Lord.

Undone before Your holiness,
Prostrate, I can but cry,
'Holy! Holy! Holy!'
Like Heaven's hosts on high.

I struggle, Lord, to speak,
Your Spirit whispers, 'Cease,
Be silent now before Your God,
Let My Presence bring you peace.'

There are no words for how I feel,
No thoughts to express my praise.
Silent now, I'll worship God,
Who is Awesome in all His ways.

2015

Another valuable lesson was learnt while preparing for a retreat entitled 'More of Him', focusing on the life of John the Baptist - a lesson on living and serving humbly. Although Jesus would say of him that 'of those born of women, there is no one greater than John', John's assessment was rather different. He referred to himself as merely a voice, one who would 'make straight the way for the Lord'. Despite having a very successful ministry, preaching repentance and baptising many followers, John was more than willing to stand aside and point to Jesus as the promised Messiah, telling his followers, 'He must become greater and greater and I must become less and less.' There was no room in John's life for resentment or jealousy of Jesus' success.

John used some beautiful imagery to define his role - that of the Bridegroom's friend:

'It is the bridegroom who marries the bride, and the best man is simply glad to stand with him and hear his vows.'

In Jewish tradition, the Bridegroom's friend had various responsibilities. He sometimes acted as the agent used by the father to search for the bride and mediate between the two families. He would have been a deeply trusted individual who had intimate knowledge of the family. He could have been used as a messenger between the future bride and groom during the betrothal and had a role in the ceremony. He stood ready to do the will of the Bridegroom and to promote the honour and pleasure of his friend. John spoke of himself as 'attending' the Bridegroom - waiting for him and listening to him, as a servant would attend his master. He was 'full of joy' at the sound of the Bridegroom's voice.

Live humbly and serve gladly - lessons that were all part of the preparation for the big change!

MORE OF HIM AND LESS OF ME

The crowds came out to hear him preach
Baptised by him to be
They heard him cry to all around
More of Him and less of me.

John searched the crowd with longing eye
The Son of God to see
He watched the Dove descend, remain
More of Him and less of me.

He heard how Jesus healed the lame
The blind were made to see
Knew in his heart his task was done
More of Him and less of me.

What lessons I can learn from John
Who served in deep humility
Resist the pride that rises up
More of Him and less of me.

I look into my heart and know
How selfish I can be
I sense the Spirit's prompt inside
More of Him and less of me.

May I be content, like John
The Bridegroom's friend to be
Wait by His side to do His will
More of Him and less of me.

So as I gaze at Christ the Lord
Before Him bend the knee
May my heart's cry ring out to Heaven -
All of Him and none of me!

2014

CHAPTER 3

WAITING FOR CHANGE

Ever since a significant encounter with God's Holy Spirit in my own home over 30 years ago and immensely grateful for how that encounter had transformed my prayer life and enriched my reading of the Bible, I had longed to see others have a similar experience. I began to pray, with some folks in the church, for God to bring about change and we began to see a new openness to the work of the Holy Spirit among us. We were greatly encouraged to see a new emphasis on worship, to hear teaching on the gifts of the Holy Spirit, welcomed the introduction of prayer ministry and valued the opportunity to join in quiet days. But change came slowly, as is often the case in churches as large as ours. And I didn't like having to wait!

During a Prayer Week in 2015, one of the themes was based on the story of Joshua and the children of Israel at the crossing of the Jordan River. They had arrived at the promised land - they could see it across the river but God's command to them was to wait. They had to camp for 3 days before crossing in order to purify themselves and receive instructions on exactly how they were to cross. I wasn't entirely sure that I wanted to hear a command to wait so I had a little conversation with God about it!

WAITING

I'm not so good at waiting, Lord,
By faith the land I see,
Can almost taste the milk and honey
You said You'd give to me.

I feel like Israel of old,
Who wandered forty years,
Camping, moving, waiting, Lord,
A journey of pain and tears.

It ended with a time of loss,
For thirty days they grieved,
I've known loss too, I'm waiting, Lord,
For my pain to be relieved.

Then, land in sight, at river's edge,
Once more You said to stay,
To set up camp, to rest a while,
And wait for a coming day.

I think that's where I am just now,
I've heard the words You said,
But I'm not so good at waiting, Lord,
I'd like to rush ahead.

I'd like to be in the promised land,
To settle there and see
The blessings of Your lavish grace
Poured freely over me.

I'd like to see my church be drenched
In the Spirit's might and power,
Filled with Your love, Your grace, Your joy,
Starting this day, this hour!

But I have heard Your call to wait,
To calm my soul, be still,
So as I wait, I'm asking, Lord,
Your peace my heart to fill.

For rain that falls on seed today
Takes time its work to do,
Just so, the Holy Spirit's rain
May grow fruit slowly too.

So make me good at waiting, Lord,
Now that the land's in sight,
May every tiny sign of grace
Be welcomed with delight.

2015

One year later, the same speaker (Pastor Jim Graham) was invited to preach again during our prayer week - we loved the gracious ministry of this Godly man and were delighted to welcome him back. When he spoke to the prayer ministry team, I couldn't believe what I was hearing - his word to us was 'Wait'. This time, however, I heard the word differently. The passage used was a familiar one - Isaiah 40 (ESV) - *'They who wait for the Lord shall renew their strength'*.

As I thought about this verse, I realised that the word 'wait' had taken on a new meaning for me - I saw it in the context of a devoted servant who wanted only to do his master's bidding, waiting with his gaze fixed on the master's face, ready to leap into action at the slightest nod or gesture. I could cope with this sort of waiting!

WAIT

You've said before to wait, dear Lord
To be calm, hold back, be still,
To consecrate myself to You,
Yield completely to Your will.

You've said to wait again, dear Lord,
But a different call I hear:
You've called me, Lord to expectation,
To hear Your voice distinct and clear.

The servant waits upon his Lord,
On Him he sets his gaze,
He listens for his master's voice
That guides him all his days.

So would I wait on You dear Lord,
Draw close to see Your smile,
Bow down to worship at Your feet
Listening intently all the while.

And as I wait, I long to know
Your powerful touch today.
I wait with eagerness and joy
Your Voice I promise to obey.

2016

Nature has many similar lessons to teach us about waiting patiently for change. Bulbs planted in Winter wait deep in the soil, all through the long dark days until Spring arrives and the flowers push their way to the surface to delight all our hearts. Trees shed their leaves in Autumn and wait naked, dark skeletons against grey skies, until fresh buds appear to clothe them once again. One cold November day I noticed a little flash of colour in the middle of a rose bed - a pale pink rose had waited for this moment to bloom - my November rose. It was a welcome reminder that even fragile things can survive the winds and storms of Autumn to bring joy to the heart of a gardener in Winter.

NOVEMBER ROSE

My beautiful November rose
Is trying hard to bloom
It brings a little colour
To a day of wintry gloom.

Its leaves curl inward on their stem
Turned brown by wind and rain,
The stalk is stripped of other leaves
That won't grow back again.

It gamely lifts its tiny head
In the shelter of the hedges,
Its petals, paler than before
Look worn around the edges.

Those petals, though, are soft to touch,
Their beauty still amazes,
Day after day they open up
And draw admiring gazes.

The fragrance from that little rose
Delights my heart each day,
It gives the same sweet perfume
In November, as in May.

We all must face November
With its winds of grief and pain,
And, like the rose, just try to bloom
Till season's change again.

For November's not forever
The sun will shine, I know,
And God will hold us close till then
He will never let us go.

So I tried to be patient as I waited and tried not to be discouraged when I couldn't see much changing and while I waited I watched and listened for any sign that the Master might give me, any indication that He was on the move.

At that stage, I didn't think it would necessitate a change in me and a change of church!

CHAPTER 4
CHANGE IN ME

Change is never a comfortable process! A little story I wrote as a response to a prompt sent out by a Writers' Group I attend takes a light-hearted look at what can be a painful process. It is based on the true story of my mother, Ruby's hat.

THE HAT'S TALE

When I was young, everyone called me Ruby's hat but now most people refer to me as Nanna's old hat. I'm a beige felt hat and I'm afraid I've lived a beige sort of life. Until recently...

Ruby bought me because I was a perfect match for the beige in her new outfit but even I knew when I first saw our reflection in the shop mirror that my beige colouring did nothing to enhance the appearance of the middle-aged, grey-haired lady who glanced anxiously from side to side to see if I suited her. She was delighted, however, with the perfect colour match and so I became Ruby's new Sunday hat.

For a while, life assumed a predictable pattern - every time the new outfit was brought out of the wardrobe, I was lifted out of the hatbox and off we went to Church. I quite liked going to Church - Ruby was an elder's wife so all the other hats looked up to me. I made sure I held on tightly to Ruby's curls - a difficult enough task considering all the standing up and sitting down involved in Church, not to mention the head bowing when she prayed! I nearly slipped forward once during prayer but just managed to hold myself together.

I used to listen to the sermons, though sometimes they were a bit boring! I did get excited, however, when I heard the preacher talk about some services that were to take place - Easter services, he called them. He sounded enthusiastic about it all and anticipation rose within me. I wanted to find out what Easter was all about.

On Easter Sunday, I could hardly contain my excitement as I waited to be lifted out of the hatbox so you can imagine my disappointment when I heard Ruby say,

'You know, I think I'll wear my new hat today - the beige one is a bit too... well, beige... a bit too dull and plain for Easter Sunday.'

Well, I spent the entire day sighing and sulking and planning all sorts of revenge! Ruby had better watch out - the next time she bowed her head to pray, maybe I wouldn't hold on too tightly - better still, I might just loosen my grip when she looked down to read - then everyone else would see as I slid slowly down over her eyes!

Unfortunately, I never got the opportunity to carry out my plan because Ruby never lifted me out of the hatbox again. And you know, I was just as disappointed at not finding out about Easter as I was at being left in the hatbox on top of the wardrobe.

The years passed and Ruby died and soon afterwards her daughter and granddaughter came to clear out her wardrobe. I had been dreading that day - I knew what happened to old hats and I had been told by the new Easter hat that very few ladies wore hats to church any more. There didn't seem to be much use for a beige hat that had lived a beige life!

To my astonishment, the granddaughter picked me out of the hatbox, muttering,

'This might be useful someday.'

She took me home and that's when I became Nanna's old hat. When the granddaughter had children of her own, I moved into the dressing up box with lots of pretty Disney dresses and shoes and somehow my life wasn't so beige anymore.

Then one day a few weeks ago, the most wonderful thing happened. The eldest girl, Emma, hunted through the dressing up box and picked me out.

'I think you'll do for the Easter Parade,' she said. As she hurried into the kitchen, I could feel the excitement rising - an Easter Parade - maybe after all these years I would finally discover what Easter was all about!

What followed was possibly the most uncomfortable, painful, puzzling but very exciting time of my life. Emma's Mum and Dad cut out a large circle of bright red material and sewed it over my crown and brim (that was the painful part). Then they cut out white and yellow petal shapes to make flowers which they stuck on to the red covering (uncomfortable but not too painful). Then they attached ribbons to me (the dreaded needle again) and set me carefully on Emma's head.

'I knew Nanna's old hat would come in handy someday,' said Emma's mum. 'It will look well in the Easter Parade!'

Next day, Emma wore me proudly on her head as she paraded into the school Assembly Hall and then sat listening as someone told the story of Easter. And what a story it was! If I had been able to cry, I might have even shed a little tear when I realised that my new decoration represented the Easter story - my red cover spoke of the blood shed by Jesus and the flowers were a reminder of His resurrection - the new life that springs forth from a seed buried in the ground.

And to crown it all (pardon the pun!) I got a new name that day - now everyone calls me Emma's Easter bonnet.

No one enjoys the process of change, whether it is a renovation, restoration or complete transformation but God promises in Psalm 23 to restore our souls and so we know that change is part of His plan for us. When I think of words like restoration, two pictures come to my mind - a carpenter in his workshop and a potter at his wheel.

HE RESTORES MY SOUL

He called me into His workshop,
His intent - to renew my soul,
To fix in my life what was broken
And send me away again whole.

I wasn't quite sure I was ready
To surrender my life to His hand,
To yield to the cleansing and shaping,
To obey His every command.

But His gaze looked deep in my soul,
Saw the damage caused by my sin,
He called forth a deep repentance
So I yielded and let Him begin.

The process was long and painful,
My thoughts and motives laid bare.
But I learnt, through the tears and the heartache
That this stripping away showed His care.

Those jagged edges of pride,
Those scratches of selfishness too
His mighty hand had to remove,
Before He could work to renew.

Each piece that was broken He mended,
My joy He restored once again,
His Spirit flowed without measure,
My soul sang a joyous refrain.

I will never be fully restored
Till He calls me to Heaven above.
But each day may I yield to His shaping,
Be restored in His Workshop of Love.

2015

When the carpenter examines a piece of damaged furniture, he sees places that are worn, places that are broken, places that need to be sanded down and places that just require waxing or polishing. His work on each damaged piece is unique. Robert and I enjoy watching The Repair Shop, a programme which shows broken or damaged pieces brought to a workshop to be repaired. We are amazed at the time and care the carpenter in the series gives to each piece and the pride he takes in revealing his finished restoration. I like to imagine that the heavenly Carpenter looks at me with such pride when I allow His Holy Spirit to work in my life. Even though the process may be difficult, the result is surely worth it!

The picture of the potter speaks more of transformation.

MOULD ME

The grey, shapeless lump of clay
Lay where the Potter threw it.
Misshapen, gone wrong, broken.
Then turned the wheel.
It seemed the clay might fly away
But all at once the Potter's hands
Secured it firmly.
His hands pressed hard to shape the clay
His thumbs pushed unrelenting
Until the stubborn clay gave way
And beauty in curve and shape appeared.

The Potter still had work to do
For curve and shape, though beautiful,
Were not enough.
The wheel continued turning

But now His hands pressed inward
Right into its very core
And once again it yielded to His touch.
And space was formed inside the clay
To make this vessel useful.

The Potter still had work to do
For usefulness and pleasing shape
Were not enough.
Soft, pliant clay would not withstand
The bruises, dents and marks the Potter knew
Would be inflicted on his masterpiece.
The flames were fanned
The furnace heat was fierce
And into the fire the Potter placed
His vessel.

But why? To burn, to utterly destroy?
Ah no - the furnace fire was only for a time
And His intent was only for its good.
For vessels that are beautiful and fit for use
Also must be strong
And strength comes only in the fire.

2016

By the time this poem was written, I was already beginning to understand something of what it felt like to be moulded by the Heavenly Potter, to be in the fire and know something of its heat. Thorny issues had to be faced, conflict was causing broken relationships and it became increasingly difficult to see how God could bring good out of the situation we were in or even if we would find the strength we needed to endure the fire. At a Quiet Day near the end of the year, I found it hard to concentrate, thoughts racing all over the place. As usual, I turned my prayer into poetry.

STILLED AND QUIETENED

My head gets very busy, Lord
With questions thick and fast,
Your Spirit flows and calms my mind
And quiet comes at last.

Whenever anger's in my heart
And hasty words arise,
Your Spirit puts a check on mine
To help my words be wise.

When I feel only helpless, Lord
There's nothing I can do
Your Spirit whispers 'Courage, child'
My hope then rests in You.

When I get disappointed, Lord
Discouraged by what's passed
Your Spirit comes to reassure
That You will hold me fast.

So fill me with Your peace, O Lord
Give wisdom from above
Still and quieten my soul
Embrace me in Your love.

2016

CHAPTER 5

JOY IN CHANGING TIMES

It would be wrong to give the impression that when life begins to shift and change, there is no joy to be found and every day is full of stress. When God has His hand on our lives, there is always joy to be found. For much of this period, life flowed on as usual. Our children had all grown up and two of them had children of their own, our six granddaughters. Obviously, the next generation has lost the recipe for boys!

Four of our granddaughters lived nearby and we found so much joy being around them, seeing their characters develop, having them over to our house for sleepovers (or should that be wake-overs?) and taking them out to visit parks and museums. Our son, daughter-in-law and our two eldest granddaughters, who had been living in Australia, came home for Christmas and we thoroughly enjoyed the noisy mayhem of numerous large family gatherings. We fitted in a few holidays and talked idly about moving house, downsizing now that the family had all moved out.

Easter has always been a time of great joy for me, especially Easter Sunday when we celebrate the resurrection and a new poem often marks the occasion. No matter what circumstances we find ourselves in, no matter how hard life is at the time, it is almost impossible not to rejoice at the thought of Jesus rising from the dead.

RESURRECTION!

Resurrection!
The woman did not recognise her Lord,
Last seen so helpless, lifeless, cold,
Laid in a grave by friends who didn't know
That Jesus Christ would rise, to break death's hold.

Resurrection!
No longer dead but gloriously alive,
No longer held within a cold, dark tomb,
No longer bearing all the sin of men,
No longer drinking from a cup of wrath and doom.

Resurrection!
No longer stripped and bleeding on a cross,
No longer crying out in awful loss
As God the Father turned away His face,
Poured out His wrath on Jesus in my place.

Resurrection!
How can my heart not burst with awe and wonder?
How can my mouth be silent? I must sing!
He is not dead but gloriously alive.
My joy, my praise, my worship I must bring.

2015

Pondering on God's glory and majesty always resulted in joy - my response to reading Psalm 8 illustrates this, inspired by another prompt supplied by the Edgehill Writers' Group.

YOU HAVE SET YOUR GLORY ABOVE THE HEAVENS.

I like to think that David wrote this Psalm at night - maybe after taking an evening stroll on the rooftop of his palace. There would have been little light pollution to spoil the splendour of the night sky above his head - a black cloth, embroidered with a thousand sparkling stars. No wonder it inspired in him this wonderful psalm of praise.

I was arrested by an interesting statement in the first verse, 'You have set Your Glory above the heavens.' David knew that the Glory of God was far above the magnificence that he could see. But David's view was limited.

Today we understand more fully the truth in David's statement - God has indeed set His Glory above the heavens, in a universe that David could not see and could never have imagined. But thanks to space travel, powerful telescopes and the Internet, we can see it in all its amazing beauty and majesty.

Did you know that in our little galaxy, the Milky Way, there are estimated to be between 200 and 400 billion stars and 100 billion planets? Did you know that in the universe, there are 1 billion trillion stars and that 275 million stars are born every day? Did you know that we are hurtling through space at over 300 miles per second - so, in just one minute, we travel at least 18,000 miles?

It all has the effect of making me feel small and insignificant. King David felt that too. 'Why does God even bother with mankind?' he asks. A good question!

But David knew a secret that you and I know too - the God who set the moon and stars in His glorious universe also set a crown of glory and honour on our heads. Why God chose to do so, I have no idea but what a difference it has made to us - made possible connection and communication and communion with the God whose creative Word produced spinning planets and breathtakingly beautiful galaxies. He has truly set His Glory above the heavens.

Joy just bubbles up when we think of these great truths! Although many of David's Psalms point to the majestic splendour of a high and holy Creator God, he also writes of God as *'my shepherd'* in the beautifully tender Psalm 23. At yet another Quiet Day, to my surprise, I found myself scribbling the words of a new 'Master' piece - I hadn't written anything in that style for a few years. Maybe I just needed to know Him as 'my Shepherd' at that moment during those changing times.

THE SHEPHERD

The shepherd led his flock along the foothills of the high mountain, while the Master and I watched from a quiet place in the valley. From time to time his voice would call out a name and a sheep that had been lagging would lift his head and come running to join the flock once more.

'He knows them all by name,' I whispered excitedly to the Master. 'How does he do that? I can't tell the difference - they're all sheep to me!'

The Master smiled. 'He cares for them,' He said tenderly. 'He has cared for them since they were born - in fact since before they were born for he cared for the mothers who carried them. He named each lamb when it was delivered, and he has watched over them every day since then. So he knows them - how each one looks, how each one walks... the ones that are likely to lag behind!'

He looked at me then and I dropped my eyes, unable to meet His gaze. I could identify with the lagging sheep - so many times I got distracted as I followed the Master. Interesting things at the side of the road caught my attention, attractive little paths called out to me to explore them or sheer laziness caused me to lag behind until suddenly I could only hear the Master's voice faintly in the distance.

'I'm sorry,' I whispered, 'I'll try to keep my focus on You, I'll try not to be so easily distracted.'

By now the shepherd on the hillside had stopped at a crossroads. He waited until his flock gathered around him and then opened a gate that led into a large, green pastureland. I laughed aloud as the sheep bumped into each other and even tried to climb over each other to get in through the gate to the rich pasture. They spread out over the field and began to feast, hungry after their long journey along the mountain path.

Then suddenly I noticed that a few sheep hadn't followed the shepherd in through the gate. Some had simply continued along the path and were trying to feed on what grass they could find along the edges, but others had followed another road that led up the steep mountainside. I turned to the Master in some dismay,

'That's such a dangerous path to take,' I cried out to the Master. 'They could so easily fall on the rocks and they won't find much food there either!'

'I know, Child,' He replied, 'some sheep just like to go their own way, to do their own thing - disobedient and stubborn. Just like My sheep - I want to lead them to green pastures and still waters but they refuse to follow My leading. But watch, My child...watch what the shepherd does!'

The shepherd, who had been resting near the gate, seemed to sense that something was wrong and went back on to the mountain path. He hurried after the sheep who had continued along that way and used his shepherd's staff to prod them back towards the gate and into the green pastures. They had just begun to graze contentedly on the rich supply of food when a bleat of distress rang out across the valley. The shepherd headed in the direction of the sound. We could just make out what had happened - one of the sheep which had scrambled up the mountainside had fallen into a deep ravine and was now bleating helplessly at the bottom. I held my breath as the shepherd hurried to the spot, lay down at the edge to assess the situation, then slowly and carefully began to make his way to the injured sheep. We could hear him calling out to the sheep by its name, reassuring it that he was close by. When he was near enough, he used the crook of his staff to pull the sheep to his side. Then he picked up the sheep and carried it on his shoulders to safety. As he made his way down, he called out to the other disobedient sheep and some lifted their heads when they heard his voice and followed him back to the path. I was sad to see that others ignored his voice or even ran away from him to continue their perilous quest for food on the rocky slopes of the mountain.

'What will happen to them?' I asked. 'Will they ever find the green pastures?'

There was sadness in the Master's eyes as He replied.

'All I can tell you, My child, is that the shepherd will keep calling and keep searching. He won't give up on his sheep.'

Once back in the pasture, the shepherd carefully examined the little sheep. It had been wounded by its fall into the ravine and I was intrigued to see the shepherd take a horn of oil from the bag he carried and bathe the wounds with the oil. The little sheep seemed to sense that the shepherd was trying to help, and it lay still on the grass and surrendered to the shepherd's hands. When every wound had been treated, he carried the sheep to the stream that ran along the side of the pasture and encouraged the sheep to drink. It did so thirstily and then, exhausted by its ordeal, stretched out and fell asleep.

I let my breath out in a rush of relief and then began to cry as I thought back over the many times I had just been like that disobedient wilful sheep, determined to go my own way, regardless of the danger.

'How I must have tried Your patience,' I whispered through my tears. 'I can't thank you enough for always coming after me, always rescuing me from the dangerous places I have gone, always carrying me when I couldn't walk on my own and always tending my wounds with Your anointing oil. Thank You from the bottom of my heart!'

I knelt in homage before the Master and at that moment, felt His hand on my shoulder and His oil begin to flow over my bowed head, pouring like healing salve into my wounds. Like the little sheep, I surrendered myself to His care. He had been and always would be my Good Shepherd who would continue to call me by name and lead me to green pastures and still waters.

CHAPTER 6

FORGIVING BRINGS CHANGE

During our last couple of years in Ballynahinch, I became concerned that there had been no women's ministry in the church where relationships could be strengthened, and new friendships formed and which would provide fellowship and encouragement for the ladies. I asked permission (which was granted) to begin what became known as 'One Another' and we began meeting together. The format was simple: a cuppa and a chat, worship, a 'Getting to know you' interview, in which we shared our stories and then each session ended with teaching on one of the 'one anothers' of Scripture. Our 'homework' each time was to put into practice that month's one another.

At the beginning of our first get together I read this poem, written that summer as I spent time in preparation for the monthly meetings. It outlined what I felt was God's heart for our little group.

TOGETHER

There's a power in together
That one alone can never know,
Designed by God to serve as one,
That's how we live and grow.

For we are joined together
Christ's Glory to display,
Shaped by some great mystery
Into His body on earth today.

And we are held together
By bonds of grace and love,
Clasping hands and linking arms
As we work for God above.

Built together, brick by brick,
Standing side by side,
Formed into a dwelling place
Where His Spirit can abide

May we have power together
To grasp and know His love
And share with one another
Blessings poured out from above.

For there is power in together
In the one another way,
Serving Him by serving others
Living together day by day.

2015

During the first year we worked our way through seven of the 'one anothers' - Love one another, Prefer one another, Accept one another, Pray for one another, Greet one another, Comfort one another and Bear one another's burdens. The ladies enjoyed our meetings together and so we agreed to continue meeting for a second year. The first two topics that year were about encouraging one another and serving one another and as usual, a good group of women came along. As I prepared for the following one, I felt it was such a relevant topic 'Forgive one Another' for our church at that time, as there were many hurting and broken people among us. I was sure that it was the most important 'one another' of all for us to put into practice, so when the turnout was significantly smaller than usual, I was disappointed. I did go home, however, content that God had spoken into the lives and situations of some of the group who were there.

On the following Sunday, I was amazed by the number of ladies who told me that they had fully intended to be at the meeting, but something happened to prevent them - so much so that I began to believe that the enemy had been at work and he didn't want people to hear about forgiveness! That thought was like a red rag to a bull and I decided there was no way he was going to win that battle! So I printed out the talk and provided copies to anyone who wanted to read it. As I saw the men of the church as well as the women take the copies and heard stories later of how they had been impacted and challenged by it, I realised that once again the enemy had overreached himself - the Lord has a way of overturning the enemy's schemes.

Forgiving certainly brings change but it can be a tough road to walk. The leaflet I prepared included the two verses on which the talk was based and also some of the material from the course we were following (Love One Another by Don McMinn):

> Ephesians 4:30 - 5:2 *'And do not grieve the Holy Spirit of God, with whom you were sealed for the day of*

redemption. Get rid of all bitterness, rage and anger, brawling and slander, along with every form of malice. Be kind and compassionate to one another, forgiving each other, just as in Christ, God forgave you. Be imitators of God, therefore, as dearly loved children and live a life of love, just as Christ loved us and gave Himself for us as a fragrant offering and sacrifice to God.'

Matthew 6:15 *'If you do not forgive men their sins, your Heavenly Father will not forgive your sins.'*

We started off by listening to the sad but true story of a married couple who had a row over how much money had been spent on sugar. They each held on to their grudge and refused to speak to each other for the next forty years! Eventually, the husband took a saw and cut their timber frame house in half, moving his half to the other side of their garden. An extreme example of the damaging effects of unforgiveness!

The first question we asked was why we find it so hard to forgive and we discovered that we don't naturally want to forgive, instead, we need the supernatural power of the Holy Spirit to forgive. Our instinct is to harbour resentment, look for revenge and never forget what has been done to us. When Paul wrote about forgiveness, he placed it in his letter to the Ephesians within the context of not grieving the Holy Spirit.

The verse in Matthew is quite possibly one of the scariest verses in the Bible! It is also one of the plainest - no excuses accepted; no wriggle room given - we must forgive!

Then we asked what is good about forgiveness and we learnt that both the forgiver and the forgiven benefit from forgiveness. The offended person is set free from anger and bitterness, which are toxic emotions that can cause untold harm, while the offender finds freedom from any emotional damage caused by their wrongdoing.

Forgiveness may even result in the restoration of the relationship - it doesn't always happen, but it sometimes does. Philip Yancey put it this way in his book, 'What's so amazing about Grace?' -

'Forgiveness offers a way out. It does not settle all questions of blame and fairness - often it pointedly evades those questions - but it does allow a relationship to start over, to begin anew.'

Finally, we asked how we do it - what it looks like. We learnt that forgiveness is a choice, an act of our will, not our emotions. We don't 'feel' like forgiving, we choose to forgive. Our forgiveness should not be dependent on whether the offender changes and we shouldn't offer forgiveness and then sulk about it! We shouldn't wait to forgive until the other person asks for it, we should just forgive - as God forgives us.

RT Kendall, in my opinion, wrote the definitive book on the subject, 'Total Forgiveness' and in it he shares seven 'proofs' that we have totally forgiven someone. They are insightful and very challenging:

1. Make the deliberate and irrevocable choice not to tell anybody what they did (he suggests if you need to tell someone for therapeutic reasons, limit it to one person who won't tell.)

2. Be pleasant to them should you be around them (do not say or do anything that would make them anxious. Put them at their ease.)

3. If conversation ensues, say that which would set them free from guilt (Guilt is most painful and we can easily punish people by sending them on a 'guilt trip.' Never do that.)

4. You let them feel good about themselves (you, therefore, must behave as though you don't even think they did anything wrong! That is hard for all of us, but it must be done.)

5. Protect them from their greatest fear (If you are aware of some deep, dark secret and fear they have, they will probably know that you know. If they can tell by your graciousness that their secret will never be revealed - ever - to anyone, they will be relieved.)
6. Keep it up today, tomorrow, this year and next (...total forgiveness is a life-long commitment.)
7. Pray for them (It is praying that God will forgive them that is, *overlook* what they have done and bless and prosper them as though they'd never sinned at all.)

Forgiveness is not an easy road - I have walked it and I know how hard it is and how much it costs. It is, however, the only Biblical response to hurt - we must forgive!

One of the many occasions, when I had to walk in forgiveness, happened in one of the schools where I taught. The principal was a man of uncertain temper and when I had to go to his office to tell him that the previous day my car had been stolen along with my bag and my school keys, instead of sympathising with me, he was furious. Following me out to the car park, he proceeded to speak very loudly - in front of pupils who were boarding the school minibus - about my incompetence, calling me irresponsible! I didn't feel that his anger was justified - after all, I hadn't asked to be robbed - but I chose to forgive his outburst and did my best to be my usual self around him. He, on the other hand, decided to deal out the silent treatment to me - which proved a little tricky as I played the piano for all the assemblies and he was forced to ask which hymns I had chosen! Calm forgiveness did eventually bring about change and at a later date, I was pleased when he asked if I would pray about a problem he was experiencing in school and of course I was happy to do so!

I'm delighted to be able to say that change has happened in our former church too and many broken relationships have been healed - forgiving does bring change. Before publishing this book, I asked Crawford Bell from the Baptist church and Ali Brown from Grace Fellowship to read the manuscript and Ali permitted me to include the following comment he made on reading this chapter.

'I can say to you with genuine joy that it has been a blessing to fellowship again with brothers and sisters in BBC, and indeed to work together on Kingdom business! Part of the healing process involved meeting with the leaders in BBC as part of the GF leadership team. Forgiveness was part of that restoration process but also self-examination, seeking forgiveness for any hurt I may have caused and forgiving self too. Self-examination, repentance and expressing forgiveness was something that both teams did before celebrating communion together. Seeking forgiveness from the other party was important. Hearing the same expressed to me was not conditional but it was both humbling and challenging.'

We kept in touch with BBC, going back to visit now and again - usually when the 'Gathering' was being held after the evening service. This is a group from various churches, led by Crawford and Clive, who meet for some fellowship, singing lots of our favourite old songs from the past and enjoying a lovely supper afterwards. I love the new songs we sing - they're the voice of today's church - but I think there is something special for each generation of worshippers in the songs that touched their hearts as they grew up. Singing a hymn from the Redemption Hymnal instantly transports me back to my childhood years in Dungannon Baptist, while one of the wonderful Gaither songs reminds me of singing them in churches all around Coleraine when we were first married - so long ago... such happy memories...

CHAPTER 7

SOME THINGS NEVER CHANGE

'Have you had any ideas about Christmas yet?' Crawford asked each year, usually near the end of the summer! Crawford is the husband of my prayer partner, Gwen.

'I'd better get my head under the duvet - I'll let you know,' was my usual rather strange response.

For many years, Christmas at the church had been marked by a special Sunday evening service the Sunday before Christmas. I had always been involved in one way or another - singing a solo, joining in a choir, playing the piano or reading a part of the well-loved story. For many of those years, the leadership had left the arranging of the service up to Crawford and me. I often found that the best time of day to mull things over and hear from the Lord was in the early hours of the morning, under the duvet - thus the rather strange conversation at the start of the chapter!

Once a theme had been agreed on, the hard work began - for Crawford that consisted of arranging carols to be performed by an amateur orchestra of varying abilities - no mean feat! To me fell the task of writing various dramas to tell the story and choosing readings for the programme. Some weeks before Christmas, Gwen would help to put up her dressmaking tables for us in their sitting room and the musical arrangements would be sorted into folders, the folders would then be distributed to the musicians, along with details of the two orchestral rehearsals - I know, I know... two rehearsals don't seem sufficient but it always worked out just fine! A choir was formed (or even cajoled!) and weekly practices were scheduled. A very helpful florist provided candles in holders, lighting and sound helpers were found, willing (and reluctant) readers were given copies of their passages, costumes were sourced, the dramas were rehearsed and a final run-through took place after morning church - lunch provided by Gwen! What a joy it was to be part of it!

Various themes were tackled over the years including Lost in Wonder, An Angel told Me and Down from His Glory. The dramas for Down from His Glory were based on a piece I had previously written for the Writers' Group, called Gloria in Excelsis Deo. I enjoyed trying to imagine what two angels in heaven might have made of the Christmas story!

Gloria in Excelsis Deo

'It's all very disconcerting,' said the most junior angel of them all, as he sat down beside the mighty archangel Michael.

'What's troubling you?' Michael asked.

'It's hard to define it,' replied the junior angel. 'There's a difference in the atmosphere up here. It's as though someone has rung a bell, and everyone knows what it means... except me. There's much more activity than usual - lots of angels with purposeful looks on their faces and groups talking together in corners. And then there's your friend Gabriel - he's been away on some mysterious special assignments. It's as though something momentous is about to happen and I'm not sure whether to dread it or be excited about it!'

Michael smiled down at the junior angel, 'Something momentous is about to happen, something that will change Earth forever.'

As he spoke, they both looked across eternity to the tiny blue sphere far in the distance and the same thought, instantly understood by the other, crossed their minds: 'Why does the great King care so much about something so insignificant and so troublesome?'

The junior angel voiced what was on their hearts. 'Something would need to change Earth forever!' he said. 'Are the warrior angels getting ready to obliterate it from the universe? Oh, I wish I could join them - how exciting that would be!'

Michael rebuked him with a stern look. 'No, it's nothing like that. The Great King has a plan to save the people of Earth, to forgive their sins.'

His companion frowned. 'But they don't deserve it - everybody up here knows how wicked they are, how selfish, how rebellious... how sinful! And the Great King is so holy He can't even look on sin, so how is He going to save them from sin?'

Michael smiled patiently at the junior angel. 'It has been planned since before the beginning of time,' he said, 'the Eternal Son is going to live on Earth.'

'The Eternal Son?' the junior angel repeated in amazement. 'He's going to live on Earth?'

Michael nodded.

'So that's what all the excitement is about - they must be getting the best robes ready and the finest crown and the most impressive escort of angels. The people of Earth will have a splendid palace for Him, I suppose?'

A fleeting, wistful look crossed Michael's face. 'No, the Eternal Son is going to be born as a human baby.'

'But He'll be born to a beautiful queen and live in a royal palace?' the junior angel insisted.

'No, He'll be born in a stable in Bethlehem, to a young unmarried girl.'

The junior angel couldn't believe what he was hearing. 'A stable - where animals live?' he questioned. 'In Bethlehem - a few houses perched on a hill? And an unmarried girl - the Eternal Son is going to be illegitimate? No, that couldn't be right!'

His look of outrage made Michael smile again.

'Don't try to understand it,' he said. 'The Great King has purposes that we can't even guess at. But I do know that it's really important that He is born to a virgin so that the people of Earth will realise that His birth is special - supernatural. They will talk of His birth for ages to come.'

The junior angel took a moment or two to think it all through and eventually gave a little nod of acceptance, satisfied that the Eternal Son would be remembered and celebrated.

'So that is why the choir has been having extra practices?' he enquired. 'I've enjoyed listening to the new song they are learning - all about Glory to God and great joy and peace on Earth. Now when the people of Earth hear the most amazing choir in the universe sing that song, they will be so impressed. The Great King will send the whole mighty host, won't He? So that everyone on Earth can hear the song at the same time? Maybe they'll have parties everywhere and bring the baby expensive gifts and...'

Michael interrupted the excited flow with a touch of his hand. 'I'm afraid not,' he said softly. 'It won't be like that. The choir will sing their song to some shepherds in Bethlehem.'

'Shepherds?' the junior angel shouted. 'Shepherds? Not kings or world leaders or army commanders or priests or prophets... to shepherds?'

He shook his head in bewilderment. 'It's not the way I would have planned it,' he said sadly. 'Will any important people be told about the birth?'

'Well,' replied Michael, 'you know the star that is soon to burst into Earth's view?'

The junior angel nodded eagerly.

'That star will be a sign in the sky to some wise men in the east.'

'Important people, are they?'

'Yes.'

'And they will bring expensive gifts for the Eternal Son?'

'Yes, gold and frankincense and myrrh.'

'Myrrh? I'm not so sure about myrrh - doesn't it have something to do with burial rituals on Earth?'

The great archangel nodded his head slowly.

'They're not going to kill Him, surely?' the junior angel asked anxiously but he could see the answer in Michael's face before the question was fully formed.

'It's not so much that they're going to kill Him,' Michael explained, 'it's more that the Eternal Son is going to offer Himself as a sacrifice.'

The junior angel's eyes widened in astonishment as understanding dawned. 'A sacrifice for sin!' he exclaimed. 'That's how the Great King is going to save them! What a wonderful plan. A sinless sacrifice - it's all beginning to make sense now!'

Michael's laugh rang out across the courts of Heaven.

'And you don't even know the best bit! The Eternal Son will defeat death and be resurrected on the third day. And millions of people on Earth will follow Him and...He'll bring them all home to Glory one day - as His beautiful bride!'

'Wow!' For once the junior angel was rendered speechless but his sparkling eyes revealed the wonder that he felt. What a plan - he could never have imagined such a magnificent plan!

'Some day,' Michael went on, 'I'll fill you in on the rest of the story but it's all beginning just now on Earth. I think I heard the first cry of a new-born baby. If we listen carefully, we might just be able to make out the song the angels are singing to the shepherds.'

And so the mighty archangel Michael settled down beside a very excited junior angel. As the strains of the angel song reached Heaven, they joined their voices to those in the skies above Earth as they sang the new song of praise,

'Glory to God in the highest Heaven,
And on Earth peace to those on whom His favour rests.'

The following year I decided to write monologues for the characters instead of writing dramas, using the theme 'Lost in Wonder'. The candle-lit church looked beautiful as usual, the musicians played with their usual enthusiasm, the monologues were sensitively performed. Everything was just as normal, wasn't it? Some things never change, and Christmas is one of them - right? I wasn't to know, even as I listened to Mary's monologue being beautifully read by a young girl, probably about the same age Mary would have been, that the following year, someone else would be sitting in my seat at the piano and I would be celebrating Christmas with a new group of believers and in a very different way.

Life was about to change! Mary knew all about changing circumstances:

MARY

I used to wonder what it would be like to see an angel. I used to wonder what he would look like, how I would react. Well, now I know - I was afraid and greatly troubled and scared of what he might say! To be honest, I found it hard to get my head around what he was telling me... I would have a son even though I had no husband... this son would reign on David's throne. That was amazing enough - and difficult to see how the son of a young girl from Nazareth could ever reign as the King...

but I found it even harder to accept that any son of mine could be called the Son of the Most-High or the Son of God. It sounds like blasphemy when I say that but that's what the angel told me.

So I waited and sure enough - it wasn't long until I began to notice the signs of a pregnancy. I had to believe it then! The hardest part was telling Joseph and seeing the pain and disappointment in his eyes. I watched him walk away and thought that I would have to do it all alone.

But God was gracious to us and sent an angel to Joseph in a dream, reassuring him that it was all part of God's plan, that the pregnancy was not natural, but supernatural, that he was to accept me into his home as his wife. So here I am, waiting anxiously for the birth of my son.

It hasn't been easy, of course - when it became obvious that I was going to have a baby, the town gossips got busy and some very unkind things were said. Some of my friends turned their backs on me - that was hard to take.

I've just returned from Judea - I went down to visit Elizabeth and stay with her for a while - it's not easy for her being so much older. Imagine the two of us being pregnant at the same time! We never thought that would happen! She still can't quite believe that she's going to have a child.

It was a long journey down to Judea - I was so glad to be back in Nazareth. So I wasn't too pleased when Joseph told me that I'm going to have to do it all over again - right at the time the baby is due! I'm not looking forward to that, but you can't argue with the Romans - if they call a census you just have to get up and go back to your home town - and Joseph's home town is Bethlehem. I wonder if that's all part of the plan too - Bethlehem was David's town and this child is to sit on David's throne... Oh, I don't know... I just have to trust God, that He knows what He is doing.

Anyway, the long journey to Elizabeth's house was worth it because the most amazing thing happened when I arrived there.

I greeted her as I normally would when she suddenly clutched at her stomach and began to shout a prophecy over me! She told me afterwards that the baby in her womb had leapt when he heard my voice. I was astonished at what she said - I didn't think she even knew I was pregnant. 'Blessed are you among women,' she shouted, 'and blessed is the Child you will bear. But why am I so favoured that the mother of my Lord should come to me?' She called my child her Lord!

As if that wasn't enough, I began to prophesy too - it was like a song rising from deep in my soul. I don't think I will ever forget the words...

'My soul magnifies the Lord, and my spirit rejoices in God my Saviour for He has been mindful of the humble estate of His servant. From now on all generations will call me blessed for the Mighty One has done great things for me - holy is His Name.'

What an amazing experience that was... I'm lost in wonder.

Another thing that never seemed to change for us was our love of family get-togethers. Christmas, Easter, weddings and lots of birthday meals filled the calendar most years but the Christmas of 2016 and the New Year that followed produced the largest family gathering to date! Our son, Julian, and his family, who had emigrated to Australia, decided to make a three-week visit home. At the same time, my brother's daughter and son-in-law and new baby son, who lived in Berlin, also returned home. Ray's son and his wife, who lived in London, also came home for Christmas. We all met in Tami and Andy's home for a noisy, joyous meal - what a gathering that was! Twenty-two of us, all trying to catch up and some cousins, uncles and aunties meeting for the first time.

That same Christmas, in 2016, I discovered an interesting theory about the shepherds of Bethlehem - it's likely they were Temple shepherds whose main duty was to rear the paschal lambs for sacrifice and of course this inspired a poem!

SWADDLING CLOTHS

The Temple shepherds watched with care
The sheep as they lay down
For these were special Temple flocks
In the fields near Bethlehem town.

No spot, no blemish was allowed
To mar their perfect beauty,
For raising lambs for sacrifice
Was the Temple shepherds' duty.

At lambing time the ewes were led
To a special birthing place
Beneath the Tower of the Flock
In a manger at its base.

Each lamb was washed with ritual care
And if no fault was found,
To keep its tiny form from hurt,
In swaddling cloths was bound.

So when the angels sang their song
Sent shepherds on their way -
Was this the place they hurried to,
Was this where Jesus lay?

And did they recognise the sign -
The cloths that held Him tight?
Did they see a Paschal Lamb
Who had been born that night?

And when that sacrificial Lamb
Hung on a Cross of shame,
Did any Temple shepherds come
To kneel and call on His Name?

I'd like to think one shepherd wise
Kept the memory in his heart
Of a baby wrapped in swaddling cloths,
Bringing peace to men on earth.

2016

I sometimes wonder if the lives of those shepherds changed after that amazing night or did life just go back to normal? I wonder did any of them hear about Jesus and His miracles and make the connection with the baby they had hurried to see in a stable in Bethlehem? On that night everything had changed for our world forever.

We didn't know it then but change for us as a family was just around the corner.

CHAPTER 8

HOPING FOR CHANGE

The Robin in my Garden

'Hi there, I've got some bread for you,' I heard Robert say one cold, wintry afternoon, as I opened the back door to call him in for his dinner.

'What on earth?' I thought, 'Who is he talking to? Has he found someone begging or taken pity on some hungry, homeless person?'

No - it was neither a beggar nor a homeless man - Robert was talking to a tiny Robin.

I watched with some amusement over the next few months as the relationship between Robert and his new best friend developed. At first, the Robin hid safely in the hedge until Robert went inside, then would dart out to claim the bread left on the grass. Robert continued his rather one-sided conversations with the Robin and was delighted when one day the Robin plucked up enough courage to leave the safety of the hedge before Robert reached the back door.

Was it a coincidence, I wondered, that so many of our Christmas cards that year featured a red-breasted Robin on the front - an entire door was decorated with Robin cards? Or was I just more aware of them because of our little friend?

Winter passed and soon the weather was warm enough for Robert to work in the garden and this new friendship reached another level. 'The Robin came down beside me where I was weeding,' Robert would report. 'He flew in and out while I mowed the lawn!' His protective instincts kicked in when he thought some of the magpies were swooping in to steal the bread and he would bang the window to scare them off.

Now, Robert has been fond of cats all his life - never happier than when he has a cat purring on his lap. He would always have tried to befriend any who made their way into our garden. No longer! The robin's secret hiding place must be protected at all costs! So a rather beautiful black and white cat who liked to stroll proudly along the wall was deemed to be 'that nasty big cat who had better not go near the Robin'.

I wondered one day if birds can talk to one another? Did a swallow or a house martin ever tell our little Robin that he didn't have to stay in a hedge in Downpatrick during the long chilly winter? Did they ever chirp a song extolling the virtues of summer days in Africa and the joys of eating super-sized insects? I wondered if the song he sang back to them made any mention of a bearded gardener who fed him titbits and chased away his enemies?

I'm glad he stays to brighten up our winter with his flash of red, glad that he's content with his lot in life, happy to fulfil the purpose for which his Creator formed him. I pray that I too will know similar contentment - happy to live the life the Creator has ordained for me and sing a song of joy even on its wintry days.

2017

The prayer with which I ended the little piece above when I wrote it in February 2017 was a cry from the heart. I wasn't feeling particularly content especially concerning the situation in the church. By this time many had left, and I had serious concerns about the direction in which I felt the church was heading. So serious were my concerns that I did something that I had never done before in over 40 years of church membership!

I wrote a paper and asked to present it to the church leaders. As it turned out, I didn't have the opportunity to present it until April but it was a good meeting - I felt that I had been heard and hoped that what I had said might make a difference and bring about change.

So I waited and watched... and hoped and prayed... but the change I was hoping for didn't come.

We celebrated Easter, as usual, that year and this time my thoughts at Easter were drawn to what I called 'the in-between' days - the days between the crucifixion and the resurrection and the days between the resurrection and the ascension. In a way, I could relate to those earlier days when the disciples were confused and anxious and uncertain of their future.

A couple of months went by and then Lavinia rang. Life changed in a moment!

THE INBETWEEN DAYS

They were strange days -
The in-between days.

Filled at first with dreadful loss
Painful memories of a Cross
Of hopes that died and bitter tears
Of disbelief and anxious fears.

They closed the door
Made fast the lock
They stayed inside
They feared the knock...
Arrested... Tried... Led out to die?

Strange days - the in-between days.
Faith at a low ebb, minds in a haze.
Then into their grief, the Lord drew near
Gave them His peace and calmed their fear.
Showed them His hands, His feet, His side,
He was alive! No need to hide!

What joy they felt -
The in-between days
Now filled with peace
And songs of praise.

For forty days, their Risen Lord
Moved among them, taught His Word
Came to see them through locked door
Made them breakfast on the shore,

Restored the one who fell from grace
Met one who doubted face to face,
He was alive! No doubt at all -
So they responded to His call.

Strange days
The in-between days
Great days
The in-between days.

The call He gave - go in My Name
For us that call is still the same.
He is alive! We'll shout His praise
For we too live in in-between days.

2017

CHAPTER 9

CHANGING LOCATION

'You've put your house on the market?' more than one person said to us when they saw the For-Sale sign in the summer of 2016. 'A house on the Saul Road - you'll have no trouble selling that!'

We thought the same and began looking around Ballynahinch for a smaller house that we could move into. A new development was being advertised in a part of the town that we liked and so after seeing the plans and being allowed to view one that had just been finished, we paid a deposit on a house in the next phase and concentrated on getting our own home ready for sale.

We tidied and cleaned inside and outside and waited for the viewers to arrive - and arrive they did! Unfortunately, most of them came, walked around the house, asked lots of questions, made positive comments about how nice it was, left with a promise to 'be in touch' but never were! One viewer made an offer that was so ridiculously low, we couldn't even consider it and so a year later, we were still waiting for the house to sell. By this stage, we had had to give up the first house we had chosen but the developer very kindly agreed to move our deposit on to another house in the same development. At times we wondered just what God was doing in this very frustrating situation.

At a conference I attended in September 2017, the worship leader introduced a song that was new to me which included the line, 'He's in the waiting'. That line struck a chord and a few days later, the inevitable poem was composed!

STILL WAITING

I'm still waiting, Lord
Waiting for the phone to ring
Listening, checking, hoping
Then checking once again
My future now dependent on a call.
I do trust You, Lord, trust Your timing
But find myself frustrated by the waiting
Confused by Heaven's slow response.
In my expectation, the call was made,
The plan was laid, the cost was paid
Instead, my vision starts to fade
And I'm still waiting.

The song I sang last week
Spoke to my anxious heart
'He's in the waiting'
I sang the line
I understood its truth
So now I'm searching for You
In the waiting.
Catching faint sightings of Your mighty hand
Working in my life.
A moment that resonates,
A verse that educates,
A comfort that compensates
For the waiting.

There are lessons I must learn
In the waiting
Words I need to hear only audible
In the waiting
Glimpses of Your face only visible
In the waiting

So I wait and You wait, Lord
For the moment that will come
The completion and perfection of Your plan
And I will wait no longer.

2017

When one of the Writers' Group prompts the following month was 'Presented Faultless', I vented some of my frustration in my response but acknowledged that there was a glorious spiritual truth to be found in those two words too.

PRESENTED FAULTLESS

Ophelia and Brian did their best last week to ruin the faultless presentation of 76 Saul Road for our viewers on Friday. While they failed in their attempt to fell any of the many trees in the garden, they did succeed in littering the entire lawn and driveway with leaves and tiny branches - not the sort of first impression we wanted the viewers to have as they walked up to the front door. As soon as Ophelia had died down, we enlisted the help of a friend to clear away the debris, only to awaken to a freshly littered lawn on the morning of the viewing, thanks to breezy Brian!

So while I tidied and cleaned and polished to achieve a faultless interior, Robert got out the lawnmower, set the blades up as high as possible and hoovered up the leaves on the lawn and the driveway! It worked! The viewing went ahead and the family who came loved the house, so much so that they phoned us the next morning to ask for a second viewing. Great! Fantastic! Except that we were on our way to an all-day conference when the call came and I knew that we had fallen short on faultless presentation inside this time - breakfast dishes in the kitchen, clothes and shoes lying around - you get the picture, I'm sure!

A few phone calls later and it was all arranged - the estate agent would carry out the viewing and our daughter would drive over to the house and do a tidy up. Tami did a great job - hid things in cupboards (we may never find them again!), folded clothes neatly, washed up the dishes and put a tablecloth on the kitchen table. She made it just in time - as she opened the door to leave, the estate agent greeted her on the doorstep.

It made all the effort worthwhile, of course, when we learned that our house was number 1 on the viewers' list - hopefully that will translate into an offer we can accept. The whole process of selling a house has reminded me just how much hard work is required to achieve that faultless presentation - our house has been on sale for over a year and after an initial clearing that included at least 10 cartons of books alone, we have prepared the house for viewing on 23 occasions - cleaning floors, polishing furniture and clearing surfaces. We have trimmed hedges, tidied flower beds and arranged for a window cleaner to come before most of those viewings. So much work. I'll be delighted when it is all over!

One of my favourite benedictions can be found near the end of the book of Jude:

> *'Now unto Him who is able to keep you from falling and to present you faultless before the presence of His glory with exceeding joy, to the only wise God our Saviour, be glory and majesty, dominion and power both now and ever. Amen.'*

When we look at our lives, we see so much that needs to be tidied up and cleared away and we might be tempted to think that it's all too much - we will never be worthy to stand in the presence of a holy God. We are right, of course, about our unworthiness but we can rejoice in His promise that one day we will be presented faultless before our God. I find that hard to imagine - standing before the unveiled glory and splendour of the God of the universe - accepted because of the sacrifice of Jesus - without a single blemish... presented faultless.

PRESENTED FAULTLESS

I know I can't escape
From Your all-seeing eye
I know You see my every sin
Each fall from grace, each tiny lie.

I'm good at putting on a mask
So others cannot see
The shame and pride behind the smile
The real and not-so-pleasant me.

How will You bear, my Lord
My sinful soul to see?
How will You, O Holy Fire
Hold back from slaying me?

My hope is in Your promise
I'll stand before Your Face
Presented faultless at Your throne
Sin covered by Your grace.

Blameless in Your Presence
Loved and accepted too
Presented with exceeding joy
Blood-washed and born anew.

2017

What we didn't realise until later was that the sale of our house was all tied up, in God's plan, with His intended change of our location. His plan was not for a move to Ballynahinch but for us to stay in Downpatrick. We had been so uncertain about the church that we found it difficult to decide until one day we were talking about it all in our kitchen and I asked Robert,

'If all the other considerations were off the table, where would you prefer to live?'

'Downpatrick,' was the instant response.

'I agree,' I said without any hesitation.

'So shall I go into the Estate agent tomorrow and ask for our deposit back on the Ballynahinch house?'

'Yes, do that,' I replied, and our location was decided!

There was still a problem of course - we still had to sell our house. Viewers continued to turn up, hopes would rise and then be dashed when no offer was made. We now had an additional problem - we had to search for a suitable home in Downpatrick! The online property pages were scoured, a list of possibilities made and then we would drive around the various locations to see if it was worthwhile asking for a viewing. By November, we felt that we had found a strong possibility and fell in love with an apartment situated close to the Quoile River. We expressed our interest but couldn't put on a firm offer. God, however, had other plans that would require a further wait on His perfect timing.

A young couple came to view our house in February (now in 2018) and put in an offer but once again we felt it was too low for us to accept. We kept it on the table, however, and continued to try to negotiate with the owners of the apartment. Eventually, after raising our offer twice, they agreed on the sale with another party, and we were back to square one! By this time it was April and when I wearily went back to trawling the internet, I came across the details of the house belonging to the young couple who had recently made an offer on ours. I liked what I saw, Robert liked it too and we phoned to make an appointment to view it.

Their house turned out to be suitable and we chatted to them at the end of the viewing, asking if we could return the following day to take some measurements and check if our furniture would fit into the rooms. The next day, when we worked out that we could fit in the furniture we needed to bring with us, we suggested to them that we swap houses. They were a little taken aback as they hadn't realised that we had kept their offer on the table - a lack of communication had caused some confusion and they had been looking at other properties! As they hadn't seen our house since February, they asked to come round the following day to have another look. We readily agreed and the next day, standing in the sunshine on our patio, we shook hands on a deal - we would each phone our agents in the morning and let them know we had agreed our sales! When we finally caught on to what God had planned, things moved very quickly. It had taken almost two years and 37 viewings in the end, but it was worth waiting for and we moved into our new wee home in June.

WORTH WAITING FOR

I thought I had it all worked out,
The when, the where, the why.
I brought my thoughts to Heaven's throne,
To the One who reigns on high.
'Your thoughts are not My thoughts,' He said,
'Be still and wait a while.'
I set aside my thoughts and plans,
I felt His love, I sensed His smile.

I thought I knew the way ahead,
The path seemed clear to me.
The beauty of that winding road
Was all that I could see.
'Your ways are not My ways,' He said,
'I'll show you where to go.
From Heaven's throne a path I see
That you can't see below.'

The purposes He has for me
I may not understand
But when the way He leads is tough,
I know I'm in His hand.
'My ways are not your ways,' He says,
'My thoughts are high above.
My purposes, worth waiting for,
Are for your good, worked out in love.'

So I will wait, though waiting's hard,
I'll be content, I'll calm my soul.
I know that I can trust my God,
'Shalom,' He whispers, 'Peace, be whole.'

2018

CHAPTER 10

CHANGING CHURCH

It all began with that phone call - the following Tuesday found me attending one of the last Praise and Prayer meetings to be held in the St Patrick's Centre. I knew very little about the meeting - who would be there or who had organised it, but I recognised some faces - friends I had met at other church gatherings. When the leader arrived, one of those friends, Anne, introduced him to me as her son-in-law, John Ashe from Journey Community Church in Antrim. I was intrigued by the way he described the church to me:

'Journey Church is charismatic and egalitarian,' he said, almost immediately on being introduced. I'm not sure if that was his usual way of describing the church he and a friend had founded a few years earlier, but God knew that those two words would get my attention! It sounded like my sort of church.

The rest of the meeting included a time of praise and a word from Scripture shared by John - all very normal - the type of meeting I had experienced many times before but then John asked us to move out to a clear space in small groups to pray. John moved over to where I was standing with a girl from the Antrim church and began to speak words of prophecy over me - not what usually happened at the end of the prayer meetings I was used to!

'You have the gift of prophecy,' he said.

I had been told this before, but I would have hesitated to define how God used me to speak into the lives of others as prophecy. Often, when I was involved in the church's prayer ministry, I would find that a verse of Scripture I had read that morning was exactly what the person I was praying with needed to hear, or I would sense an urge to contact someone and find that they needed a listening ear. So I sort of bent my head in acknowledgement that it might be so.

'You have a speaking gift,' he went on.

I was able to give a more decisive nod to that statement as I had been speaking for many years in all types of churches and women's groups. I enjoyed everything about it - the moment (often under the duvet in the early morning!) when God would 'download' a theme into my heart, the preparation for the talk, the fellowship with those who had gathered and most of all, the moments of stillness when I just knew that the Holy Spirit was moving - heads would nod and eyes begin to glisten with tears. Then John added something else that surprised me.

'You know, I don't say this to everyone, but I think you will be significant in Downpatrick.'

I went home that night with lots to think about and share with Robert and with those words ringing in my heart - 'significant in Downpatrick' - could it be so?

After much prayer and heart-searching and beginning to realise that although we didn't want to leave the church in Ballynahinch, we probably couldn't stay, we decided to spend the summer months visiting other churches nearby and also take the opportunity to visit the Journey Community Church in Antrim. This was particularly important for Robert, who hadn't been able to attend the Praise and Prayer meetings due to work commitments. I wasn't sure how Robert would find the charismatic nature of the service - he was inclined to be a little (or a lot!) more reserved than me.

So, feeling a bit apprehensive, we made our way to Antrim Grammar School where the church was meeting at that time. The first thing that impressed us was the welcome we received at the door - smiling faces offering sweets and hugs! We took our seats near the back and before the service began, folks continued to come over to say hello. The worship was uplifting, and the sermon was preached by a woman, confirming the egalitarian emphasis of Journey. Robert's remark at the end of the service went a long way to helping us see Journey as a potential home church for us:

'You know, I felt very much at home - I felt free to stand or sit during worship and if I had wanted to, I could have moved around - I enjoyed it.'

There was certainly a sense of freedom and what spoke into my heart was the ease with which people went forward for prayer at the end of the service. I remember thinking,

'This is what I have been praying for in our church, what I have been longing to see!'

We went back a few times over the summer - at one of the services, Robert even felt comfortable enough to go forward for prayer - we both did but it was more of an unusual step for Robert! There was just one potential problem in my mind. It wasn't long before I realised that Journey Community Church had an association with the Bethel Church in Redding in America. I had heard and read some very strong criticism of this church, though years before I had read and been greatly blessed by one of Bill Johnson's books. Now we were considering joining a church where teams of young people from Bethel were welcomed each summer and where many of its interns were invited to serve. I knew that any decision to join Journey might well invite similar criticism. So what was I to do?

I have always preferred to judge for myself, so I began watching and listening and engaging with the young people who were in Antrim that summer. I saw them serve, I heard them pray and I watched them worship. I recognised their deep passion to know the Father's heart and to follow Jesus closely.

Then I heard of a forthcoming conference being organised by Journey, at which the main speaker would be Danny Silk, one of the leaders of Bethel Redding so I took the opportunity to go along and experience what it would be like to sit under his ministry. I found him to be a gracious, Godly man and enjoyed listening to him. Maybe not all of that strong criticism was justified?

We were also getting to know the little group who had been meeting in previous years to pray for God to move in the town of Downpatrick. We met the leaders, Fiona, Tucker, who worked for Youth Initiatives in the town and Sharon, whom we already knew through earlier days in our church. We listened to their stories and sensed their passion for the people in Downpatrick and began to feel God tug at our hearts too. For years we had lived in Downpatrick but our whole spiritual focus had been on Ballynahinch. Maybe it was time to change that focus?

Over the next few months, as we thought, talked and prayed, we gradually came to realise that not only had God unsettled us concerning staying in our current church, He was calling us to throw in our weight with this new potential work in Downpatrick. A verse in Mark chapter 2 resonated with me as I listened to God's voice in His Word:

'New wine calls for new wineskins.' (NLT)

The Journey church felt to me like a new wineskin - our decision was made.

We were anxious to leave 'well' - in good standing with the church we had loved and served for so long. So we began the painful process of leaving. I met the pastor to explain our decision, we told as many of our close friends as possible personally, I said a sad farewell to the One Another group and we gave in our resignation, which was read out at the members' meeting. It felt like the end of an era.

A few days earlier, we had taken a day trip to Portstewart, to walk the Strand and see the waves rolling in. This place has always been a 'happy place' for me, and it didn't fail to lift my spirits once again. As I returned from my walk, a beautiful rainbow appeared in the sky and the Father spoke tenderly to my aching heart.

A BEAUTY FROM THE SEA

I walked today on silky sand
Beside the singing sea
November breezes cooled my cheek
While the sun shone down on me.

The distant headland disappeared
Blue sky turned sullen grey
The breakers rolling down the strand
Grew trails of salty spray.

I changed direction, quickened pace
Fled the approaching rain
A dark cloud swallowed up the sun
So I quickened pace again.

But then a beauty from the sea
In multi coloured hue
Rose up to arch across the sky
A curve of purple, green and blue.

No rainbow forms unless the rain
Is falling from the sky
And darkest clouds can best display
The rainbow soaring high.

I walked today on silky sand
Beside a stormy sea
Felt safe beneath the rainbow's curve
That shimmered over me.

The rainbow spoke to me today
But not of pots of gold
It spoke of mercy, love and grace
God's promised peace foretold.

For storms will come, of that I'm sure
And clouds turn steely grey
But beauty rises from those storms
And calms my heart each day.

2017

There was, of course, no actual 'church' to attend in Downpatrick so we decided to join in with the morning services being held by Grace Fellowship Church in one of the schools in Ballynahinch. As it consisted mainly of former members of the Baptist church we had just left, we knew lots of people and were warmly welcomed to their services. We made it clear that we wouldn't be staying there and explained the situation in Downpatrick. We were very graciously encouraged just to rest with them for a while and we were glad to do so. This was a period I would later refer to as 'in-between'.

IN-BETWEEN

We walked away. We left.
And now we're in-between.
Between churches,
Between locations,
Between theologies,
Between friends.

We left behind
Responsibilities
Ministries
Needs
Memories.

The last car has been parked
The last prayer has been prayed
The last talk has been given
The last song has been sung.

Herein lies loss.
Loss of deep and valued friendships,
Shared laughter,
Shared tears,
Shared worship,
Shared moments of wonder.
Loss hurts.

But when He called
He spoke of new wine,
Rich and ruby-red
Ready for outpouring.

New wine calls for
New wineskins.
Newly fashioned,

Newly formed,
Newly shaped,
Newly poised
For the outpouring.

Father, give us grace
As we submit to the making,
The forming, the shaping.
Grant us patience as You fashion us,
Courage as you change us,
Hunger as you teach us,
Your Presence as You lead us
Down unfamiliar paths,
New ways of worship,
New spheres of service.

Excite us by the vision
Of the outpouring.
Your Spirit free to do His work,
Your Son's Name lifted high,
Your love embodied and released,
Blind eyes seeing,
Deaf ears hearing,
Lame feet dancing,
Lost souls seeking!

For now, the 'on hold' button
Has been pressed.
And while we wait
We need You.
Reassure us of Your nearness
In the pause,
And grant us peace for the waiting
In the in-between.

Mark 2:22
'New wine calls for new wineskins.'

CHAPTER 11
CHANGING MINISTRY

There is a grieving process that takes place when former ministries are stripped away - as I wrote in the poem at the end of the previous chapter, 'loss hurts'. I had been so involved in the Baptist church - serving in prayer ministry, leading worship, playing the piano, leading the women's group and running the occasional Quiet Day. Suddenly, everything had gone, and I felt the loss quite keenly - it felt very strange to have little to do and no part to play! Maybe things would be different when the new church was up and running...

There was great excitement when the leaders announced at one of the Praise and Prayer times (now being held in Fiona's house) that we would soon have a place to meet - arrangements had been finalised for us to rent a property in the centre of Downpatrick. At last - something to do! The building had been used as a Bingo hall and needed significant renovation to change its use into a church. So when hearing Hadden Wilson preach at Grace Fellowship Church and challenge us to answer the question, 'What are you and God working on at the moment?' my answer was 'God and I are painting window frames just now!' It was a different way to serve but I remembered the lesson I had learnt from the life of John the Baptist - live humbly and serve gladly - so I was content to put on the painting clothes and wield a paintbrush.

Looking back at that period since making a connection with Journey, I can see that there had been hints now and again that my ministry was going to change. On many occasions when

I attended services or conferences, I would find myself being given an opportunity to minister to someone - but always in a one-to-one encounter. I gave a word one Sunday in the Antrim church (with some trepidation, I might add!) and when the service was over, a lady came to me in floods of tears to tell me that the word had spoken right into her situation. I had met her briefly once before and so knew a little of her story and was able to have a chat and pray with her as the school hall was being cleared all around us.

Another occasion was significant for me - at the Danny Silk conference mentioned in an earlier chapter, one of the seminars I attended was led by Father Colomba, a young priest who has an amazing ministry in Londonderry. I wanted to thank him afterwards and so joined the line of people waiting to speak to him. There were still a few folks sitting in the seats and suddenly one of them beckoned to me to join her and her husband. As I got closer, I could see that the man was in tears. I sat down beside them, and the lady explained why she had called me over. Introducing herself as Kathy, she said,

'I remember you from the conference you took with Carol Herron some years ago. Would you pray with Andy, please? He can't stop crying and we don't know what's wrong!'

I did know what was wrong - I had been in the same seminar and had been moved by what had been said but I had also experienced unstoppable tears like Andy's in a seminar some years earlier and recognised what God was doing.

'You're praying for Ireland, Andy - God is revealing His heart for Ireland to you!'

As Andy continued to weep, Kathy told me that they had already moved to an area in the west, near the border and that they felt God was calling them to a cross-cultural ministry in that place. I had the privilege of praying into their situation and then someone from the Antrim church came over and prayed too. We have kept in touch and have become friends since then and God is blessing their work in that area. Another one-to-one encounter!

The months from December to April flew past in a flurry of busyness - painting and more painting, helping to lay carpet tiles, moving chairs from one place to another and then back again. But in the middle of all the hustle and bustle, I had a one-to-one encounter of my own. We met each week for a time of teaching and prayer and at the end of one of those meetings, I left the small room where we were meeting to find John and ask him to pray for me. He was in the large main room where the church would eventually hold the services. The men had been working hard - the floor was littered with pieces of wood and sawdust - but John began to pray and there in the middle of all the mess, I experienced a touch from the Holy Spirit and would have ended up on the floor in the sawdust had John not supported me. I tried to put it into rather inadequate words later:

YOU CAME

You came in the ordinary
In the midst of dust and noise
And men at work,
You came.

Your touch was gentle
As in times past -
The warm embrace of a much-loved Friend,
Familiar, reassuring,
The well- remembered sense of Presence.

Your touch was powerful
Rocking my stable world,
Upsetting equilibrium,
Hinting at a power divine
Too great for human frame,
The felt reality of Presence.

Your voice was clear
Speaking the Father's heart to mine,
Words of promise dropped from Heaven,
The cup I held You filled to overflowing,
Manna for my soul, honey for my lips,
Promised in Your Presence.

Your gift was peace
Deeply restful stillness,
Persistent gently flowing river,
Filling every anxious space,
Defeating every fearful thought,
Calming every restless urge.

The Peace and Promise that You give
I know are not for me alone -
A conduit, a carrier I would be
To share what flows from Heaven's throne.

2018

The experience was a reassuringly familiar one which reminded me of the first time the presence of the Holy Spirit had made my knees buckle - at a conference led by John and Carol Arnott in Mosney many years earlier - the same amazing sense of peace flooding my soul. Whatever else might change in this new adventure with God, I was grateful that He had shown me that His Spirit's way of ministering to me was (at least for now) the same as always. That first time in Mosney, I had searched in vain for words to describe the experience - in the end, I called it indescribable!

THE INDESCRIBABLE

How can you describe the indescribable
Put a name to the Presence of the Lord?
How can you explain the inexplicable?
Not by picture, not by song, not by word.

There are just no words to describe Him
All His glory, all His power, all His joy.
No explanation could ever explain Him
We can only receive and enjoy.

If I sang a song for eternity
Used an angel's tongue for my song
Even then I could never express
All the praise that to Jesus should belong.

Yet, though these words are inadequate
My lips unclean to even call Him Lord
I will tell of His grace and mighty love
And proclaim the beauty of His word.

Part of the prophetic word John spoke over my life that day was that I would be 'a carrier of peace' - what a privilege to be called to carry His peace to others! What an honour to serve Him in this way, not up front to large groups but in one-to-one encounters. Not only could I experience the 'peace whatever' I had known at the beginning of the process, I could also share that peace with others.

CHAPTER 12

BRINGING CHANGE TO DOWNPATRICK

15th April 2018

The old Bingo hall had been transformed. New walls had been built, old walls had been painted, a sound desk was installed, microphones and musical instruments were set up, the chairs were arranged to accommodate as many people as possible - everything was ready for the first service of Journey Community Church in Downpatrick. The church was packed, the worship was enthusiastic but for me, one of the highlights was when John Ashe gave an account of his call to plant a church in Downpatrick, a town where fourteen previous attempts to do so had met with limited success. I have asked John to tell the story in his own words:

The original conversation happened when Rachel and I met up with Clive and Fiona, who had been our small group leaders in CFC (a Christian Fellowship Church in Belfast). They had moved down to Downpatrick and Fiona always had a heart to see a similar church in the town. They were friends with a group from CFC who had tried to plant a church there, but I don't think it survived. So it was they who had put it on my radar - they were down there praying.

When we started the Journey Community Church in Antrim, we brought a group of young people down to pray for them - I had no intention of planting other churches at this point - didn't really have an inclination to do any of that. The young people began to prophesy a lot about churches and what God was doing and where they were going and that heightened my awareness.

Then a group of people got chatting about it all, Rachel's mum and dad (Anne and Edwin) moved to Downpatrick, and other people we knew got involved too. Clive and Fiona started coming up to Antrim, along with Tucker and a few other guys from Youth Initiatives. They were coming up to Journey, checking it out, seeing what was going on and we began to talk about what it might look like to plant a church in Downpatrick. Again, though, I never really thought much about it and didn't do anything about it.

Up to this point in my life, I have had three angel visitations - two of which are on public record and one which I'm holding on to myself for a while! The first one was either in 2005 or 2006. An angel visited me in my bedroom and took me into a prophetic dream where I saw an old galleon ship - it was moving on the sea - it had no engine, it had no sails and it was coming into a bay. I knew the bay was Ireland but the ship hit the rocks and exploded into a thousand pieces - the pieces became fireballs and I found myself looking down from a google map position, down onto Ireland, as bits of this fire began to fall all over Ireland. Originally, I thought it was revival, but I woke up and felt the Lord was saying it was a movement later on. What was interesting about this whole experience was that my face burned the next day. When I woke up, Rachel said, ' Your face is sunburned... are you OK?' There was a mark on my face, and I felt that God was speaking about a movement that He was going to establish.

The next visitation took place some years later. It was the same angel, I think - behind the curtain, with a shofar and again I was put into a prophetic dream. This time, I was standing on top of St Patrick's grave (at Down Cathedral) and I could see all around but as I looked down beside the grave, there was a headstone with a white marble plaque on it. I couldn't read it because it was in a foreign language (Latin), but I remembered the date, 1784. That date was etched into my mind at the time, but I thought no more about it.

About a month or two later, I was doing some work in Downpatrick so I called round and had a wander around the graveyard, looked for that headstone but couldn't find it anywhere. Then about a year later, during the conversations with Clive and Fiona, Rachel's parents and a few other people, I went down again. At the bottom left-hand side, down in the bottom corner, I noticed that a fallen tree had been cleared up and the ivy removed from the wall and I saw a gravestone set into the wall of the cemetery - it was the only gravestone that was in the wall. I went down, scraped back the ivy and there was the white plaque with that date on it! I remember sitting down and being gobsmacked!

The translation of the plaque reads like this:

I was Eliza
Virtue lives on after the grave
Her age 46   She died 12 October
The year of our Lord 1784

I then shared this with Rachel's mum and dad on the following Sunday. Edwin began to do some research into this gravestone, and he managed to get his hands on a book which gave him some information on Eliza Trotter and her husband, William. Among other things, William was an agent for the Southwell Estate (a position like a mayor or governor), a magistrate and a church warden at Down Parish Church - an important man in Downpatrick. He and Eliza built and lived in a large house in Irish Street, with their nine children. They were friends of none other than John Wesley, whom they invited to preach in Downpatrick. Wesley visited the town four times and on his first visit, he preached in the Grove beside the ruins of Down Cathedral and also in the new Methodist meeting house in Saul Street, which had just been opened the previous year.

The interesting part of that story was that despite their involvement with the Anglican church, they were enthusiastic about the new Methodist movement - part of its mission was to protect the Catholic landowners from the Protestant pillaging that was going on at that time. William also gave land for a new Catholic church to be built and his second wife, Frances, laid its foundation stone in 1787. I thought it was all really interesting and I suppose in many ways, that was the start of the journey.

I began looking at what it would mean to plant a church down there. We then ended up starting prayer meetings after that. The elders weren't all that sure about whether we were ready to do this yet but I felt the Lord was in it and we started a prayer meeting (with an eclectic group!) meeting in the St Patrick's Centre for a year. We then began to look for a building and we looked at various options until one day Andy (who was involved with Youth Initiatives) said, 'You know, the old Bingo Hall's just down in the centre of the town?'

I didn't know anything about it, so we contacted the estate agent. It had been sitting empty for a while.

We went down and saw it and now we're in that building! We spent a lot of time fixing it up and we spent a considerable amount of money on it. It is now fully paid off and that's pretty amazing! The church has flourished ever since. I just think the Lord's hands on it, that He knows He's on it and we know He's on it - so far, so good.

Community has always been at the heart of the Journey church and one of John's recurring challenges in his teaching during the early days of meeting together in preparation for the opening was to get out of the church building and into the community.

'Go and join something,' he was fond of saying. My response to this challenge was to enquire about volunteering with the Fountain Foodbank, a cross-community initiative run from the local Presbyterian church and founded by one of its members, Shirley Lennon. I enjoyed working with the other volunteers and serving as one of the 'meeters and greeters' once a month. I got to see the need in our town, heard many sad tales and had the privilege of praying with some of the folks who came for food parcels.

Then Robert and I were contacted by Winston Shaw who ran the local Christians Against Poverty team, asking if we would be interested in becoming befrienders for CAP in Downpatrick. After some consideration, we agreed and began accompanying the debt coaches as they helped people who found themselves caught in the debt trap. We were invited into their homes and once again, had the privilege of praying with them and encouraging them on the tough journey out of debt.

In the church we volunteered for the Welcome Team - having appreciated so much the welcome we had been given to the Antrim church, we were keen to pass it on! What a joy it has been to wait at the open door, smile a welcome, offer a sweet, invite them to have a cuppa before the service and introduce strangers to some of the Journey folks. We also tried to join in the Tuesday cleaning mornings, tidying and hoovering after the Sunday services.

It was all very different from the upfront service I had been used to in previous churches and it took a bit of getting used to - serving by cleaning toilets rather than leading worship! But God had already prepared me by teaching me to 'live humbly and serve gladly' so I tried to do just that. I wasn't needed in the worship teams - so many gifted young people were able to lead us into the Presence of God and I loved their passion and commitment. There were no ministries I could get involved in and for a while I struggled to see what my role might be.

Then one Sunday, at the end of the preservice prayer, Sharon, who was responsible for the Prayer Ministry in the church, asked if I would join the team that morning - I was honoured to be asked. I have learnt so much by ministering alongside the others in the team, especially about standing back and allowing the Holy Spirit to do His work. I was a little apprehensive at the beginning - the others seemed to flow so easily in their prophetic gifting and even wondered now and again if I should continue with it. I mentioned how I felt to Ian (the co-founder of Journey) one Sunday after his preaching had led to many coming forward for ministry and God spoke powerfully to me through his response,

'I love seeing you come forward to minister... I see you clothed in a robe of authority... and a crown on your head...'

So each time I step forward to pray with folks at the front, I ask God to clothe me in His authority and put a crown on my head and that has made a significant difference. It is, of course, a one-to-one ministry (or two-to-one) and I'm grateful that I seem to have found the place God has for me in the church. There is a lot of brokenness in our little group and it is amazing to be able to pray into the brokenness and see God change lives and situations.

For the first few months, the little church kept a low profile, but the summer programme changed all that - 'I ❤ Downpatrick' ran for a week in July and what an impact it made in the town. A team from the Last Leaf organisation in America came to help run the busy programme - a kids' club in the morning, litter picking in local estates in the afternoon, face painting and inflatables in the square in the evening and a youth programme in the late evening. Everything was free - a fact that impressed those from the community who came to see what was happening and provided a great opportunity to say why we were running this event. It was exhausting - but so worth it!

Change would come to this special place - Patrick's town - one small step at a time.

CHAPTER 13

CHANGING MINDSETS

By October I was feeling comfortable enough to give a word occasionally in our new church. I had been reading through the Gospels again and when I came to the familiar story of Jesus feeding the five thousand, I felt that there was a truth in that story that I needed to share at the Sunday service. I wrote it up later as a devotional for the next Writers' Group.

IN PRAISE OF MEAGRE LUNCHES

My reading that morning was in John, the story very familiar. I've known the story of the feeding of the 5000 for about 60 years now but that morning God showed me something new. I was arrested by Andrew's response to the little boy's offer of his lunch,

'What good is that with this huge crowd?'

It struck me that what Andrew spoke of so disparagingly was the very thing that moments later Jesus would use miraculously to feed 5000 people. I wondered how Andrew felt as he served person after person and saw the bread and fish multiply before his eyes?

I wondered too how often I had asked the same question, 'What good is that?' or even 'What good am I?' I realised that at the very moment Andrew voiced his scepticism, everything God required for the miracle was already in place - the boy's lunch had been prepared, he had made the journey to hear the Teacher, he had been noticed by Andrew, he had willingly offered his meagre lunch, the disciples were in place to distribute the food and Jesus was there to perform the miracle.

I wondered how often I forget that God is into multiplication. We might be small in number, but God multiplies our service, we might have little to give Him, but God multiplies our offering. Sometimes, even as we ask, 'What good is that?' God is already poised to work a miracle.

I've seen Him multiply this little moment of insight in the past couple of weeks - I felt first of all that it was a word for the new church plant I attend in Downpatrick and I was able to encourage them with it the following Sunday; a dear friend, now in her 80s, felt down and worthless a few days later and I was able to encourage her with this same word; I read it to a small prayer group I attend and it encouraged them to know that God can use their efforts in prayer, and here I am, tonight, using it again by reading a poem I wrote in response to it - In Praise of Meagre Lunches! I hope it will encourage you to think again when you're tempted to ask, 'What good is that?' Just give Him your meagre lunch and watch what He will do with it!

WHAT GOOD IS THAT?

Jesus watched them as they came
From near and far away.
Five thousand people gathered round
To hear what He would say.

Andrew stood there by His side
And heard the Master ask,
'How shall we feed these hungry ones?'
It seemed too great a task.

A little boy had also heard
And offered up his food
He gave it all to Andrew -
It might do someone good.

Andrew saw the meagre lunch -
Two fish, five loaves of bread
And hasty words rushed from his mouth
'What good is that?' he said.

He didn't know what Jesus knew -
God's plan was now complete.
For He would multiply the bread
And everyone would eat.

I sometimes think as Andrew thought
'What good is that?' I'll say.
'The need is great, I'm weak and small
All I can do is pray.'

I need to learn as Andrew did -
God multiplies the small
So, willingly, with open hand
I'll offer Him my all.

The prayer I offer up in faith
May be all He needs today
To work a miracle of grace -
So I'll bow the knee and pray!

2018

A mindset that asks, 'What good am I?' is a mindset that needs to change! Another mindset that needs to change is the one that results in the sleepy-headed, 'I can't be bothered, someone else can do it ' response to serving and obeying God. Meditating on a call to the church to awaken inspired another 'Master' piece soon afterwards.

THE DORMITORY

The sign on the door simply said 'Dormitory'. The Master motioned to me to enter and I obeyed, curious to see what was on the other side of the door. It was a long, narrow room, stretching far into the distance. The room was lined with beds of various shapes and sizes; ornate four-posters piled high with pillows and blankets; comfortable divans covered with colourful duvets; iron frames on which rested thin mattresses and single sheets. And in each bed lay a sleeping occupant.

I turned to the Master in bewilderment, 'What am I looking at?' I asked.

His eyes were sad as He looked along the lines of beds.

'My sleeping Church,' was His quiet reply.

'They're sleeping?' I whispered. 'Don't they know about the enemy and the battle going on outside? How can they sleep?'

Just then I heard a ringing noise, then another and another. And one by one, hands reached out from under the blankets or duvets to press a button on the clocks beside each bed and the alarms were silenced. The Master looked even sadder.

'My Spirit keeps on sounding the alarm but many just switch off and refuse to respond.'

He moved across to one of the nearby beds, leaned over to speak into the occupant's ear and said loudly,

‘Wake up, Child, the enemy is at the door!’

But His sleepy child just snuggled deeper into the duvet and pulled the pillow over her ear to drown out the Master’s voice. When the Master tried to shake her awake, she could be heard muttering lazily,

‘Leave me alone, I’m trying to sleep... It’s so warm and comfortable... Sure, someone else can deal with the enemy... someone stronger than me...’

As her voice trailed away into silence, the Master reluctantly left her bedside. I looked away, distressed by the depth of sorrow on His face and noticed some movement, far away in the middle of the room. As I moved closer, I became aware of a sound, a sweet sound, a compelling sound, a beautiful movement of chords and harmonies, soft and mysterious.

Some of the sleeping Church had heard the sound too and were leaving the comfort and warmth of their beds to form a circle in the middle of the room. As they responded to the rhythm of the music, some held each other’s hands and moved as one, others dropped to their knees as though bowed by grief while a few lay sobbing on the floor.

‘What is that sound they are responding to?’ I enquired.

The Master smiled as He told me it was the call to prayer.

‘The call can be heard at any time of day or night but so few respond to it,’ He explained.

As I watched, those in the circle began to cry out, pleading passionately for the Father to hear their petitions and to be pleased with their praise and adoration. And something that looked like smoke rose from the centre of the circle.

‘Oh, something’s wrong,’ I called out to the Master. ‘Something’s on fire! Come quickly before they are all destroyed!’

The Master began to laugh.

‘Oh you’ve got it all wrong - that’s not smoke from a fire - that’s the sweet incense of their prayers rising to the Throne Room.’

And sure enough, the more they prayed and the more passionate their requests, the more incense rose and the more its sweet fragrance filled the room. I would have liked to stay there but the Master beckoned me on. As I glanced back, I thought I caught a glimpse of mighty angelic warriors surrounding them, great celestial beings of light but even as I caught that fleeting glimpse, they had gone and I wondered if I had just imagined it.

‘The angel of the Lord encamps around those who fear Him,’ the Master answered my unspoken question. ‘It’s a circle of protection sent from the Father - the enemy often attacks those who are awake enough to pray.’

Suddenly yet another sound echoed through the dormitory - a loud rumbling and an explosive bang, followed by a flash of light. And it seemed to me that this explosive sound came in direct response to the passionate prayers that had been sent up to the Father. As more prayers ascended, another explosion boomed out, right beside the bed of one of the Master’s sleeping followers. He sat bolt upright in his bed, flung back the covers and stood unsteadily to his feet, a dazed look on his face.

A moment later, he saw the Master and ran to bow at His feet.

‘I heard Your call,’ he cried as tears ran down his face. ‘I’m Yours. Use me as You please. Send me where you will.’

The Master smiled, then took from His belt a horn of oil, anointing oil. He poured it out over the young man’s head as he lay, now prostrate, at the Master’s feet. He remained there in complete surrender for a long time as the Master smiled and the oil flowed. Then he rose to his feet, a look of utter determination on his face and marched in the direction of the door at the other end of the room.

My heart was fearful for him - he looked so young, so weak, so vulnerable - no match for the wily enemy beyond the door. But then he stepped over the threshold and what I saw before the door closed brought me great comfort. He seemed somehow taller, stronger and he was clothed in the most amazing armour of righteousness, truth and peace. From his shoulders flowed a dazzling garment of praise, in his hand he wielded the mighty sword of the Spirit and emanating from him was wave after wave of love and joy.

And I was filled with hope that one day this young follower of the Master would return to the Dormitory to send forth a clear, piercing, clarion call that would awaken the sleeping Church, deliver those held captive by the enemy and bring great joy to the heart of the Master. His joy would be echoed by those mighty warrior angels and rejoicing would resound in The Father's House.

Awake, oh sleeping Church!

2018

As I completed that piece, I found myself identifying the young follower in the story with Tucker, one of the Downpatrick leaders. I felt sure that he would be used mightily to awaken God's sleeping church wherever he was placed.

That Christmas marked a change in my mindset about how the Incarnation should be celebrated in church - no well-prepared Christmas programme this year - instead, a big community event called 'A Walk through Bethlehem', organised by Tom and Brooke, a lovely, hard-working American couple who had been seconded to serve in our wee church. It was a live nativity, complete with angels, shepherds, kings, real animals and lots of straw - so much straw that we were still hoovering it out of the carpet tiles many months later! It was an amazing, noisy, chaotic day but hundreds of people from the community came to see it, heard a simple Gospel message and were given an invitation to learn more about Jesus.

Some folks took up the opportunity to learn more about Jesus in the new year by joining us for the Alpha course which ran until the end of March. Quite a few of those who attended came into a new relationship with Jesus as a result of that course, including a friend who had come with me. She has significant issues with anxiety but often tells me of the difference it has made to have the Lord in her life - a new peace and a different way of approaching problems - a new mindset!

Sometimes even our mindset about God Himself needs to be changed and reading a verse in Romans 5 caused a little tweak in how I thought about God - primarily I referred to Him as Father or Creator or Sovereign Lord but this verse challenged me to enlarge my thinking:

> *'But now we can rejoice in our wonderful new relationship with God because our Lord Jesus Christ has made us friends of God,'* (NLT)

I was filled with joy as I wrote a response which I shared later that week with Lavinia, Gwen and Pat when we met to pray together. Just imagine - we're friends of God!

HIS FRIEND

My faith is placed in Jesus Christ
Made righteous in God's sight
Snatched from Satan's kingdom
Into the Father's light.

I don't deserve this privilege
A daughter of the King
Knowing I share His Glory
Just makes my spirit sing.

When hard times come - they always do!
Faith helps me hold on tight
I think of Jesus on the cross
My suffering then seems light.

I can rejoice in grief and pain
When He fills me with His love
The Spirit freely pours it out -
Gifted from Heaven above.

But what astounds me most of all
Is that I'm called His friend
Bound as friends with Father God
A love that will never end.

Now, I could be a better friend
Draw closer day by day
His friendship never wavers
He's my Friend, all the way.

2019

CHAPTER 14
DESIRING CHANGE

> Ecclesiastes 3: *'For everything there is a season, a time for every activity under Heaven... God has made everything beautiful in its time. He has planted eternity in the human heart, but even so, people cannot see the whole scope of God's work from beginning to end.'* (NLT)

The small ugly little bulb had very little going for it in September when I brought it home to plant in my garden, but it was bursting with God-given potential. Everything that was needed to produce the gorgeous yellow daffodil was contained inside the bulb. Sometimes we look at ourselves and see only smallness or ugliness - we don't realize that we too are bursting with God-given potential to produce the beauty of His Grace and to demonstrate the loveliness of His Glory to our world.

What the bulb required for its transformation was darkness and time. We don't usually appreciate periods of darkness in our lives and most of us don't like waiting but often these are the ways God chooses to change us into the likeness of His Son. There are roots to be put down in the darkness that will nourish us for years to come, treasures to be discovered that can come no other way and strength to be increased as we push upwards toward His light. These are all slow processes that take time... time that is well spent.

For just as a Spring daffodil delights the heart, so too will a transformed follower of the Master delight the heart of God and the hearts of all who cross his path. So be patient and allow Him to do His work... He makes everything beautiful in its time!

When I was invited to speak at a Ladies' Daffodil Tea, I thought of that wonderful verse in Ecclesiastes, based my talk around it and wrote the poem that follows especially for them. I had never been to a daffodil tea before but thoroughly enjoyed the experience! There were daffodils on every table on which a sumptuous afternoon tea had been spread and the ladies who had gathered chatted happily together as they ate. I had brought a daffodil bulb with me and used it to challenge the ladies to realise the God-given potential that was within each of them.

BEAUTIFUL IN HIS TIME

The bulb was planted in September
No beauty to be seen at all
Round, hard, ugly, dry
Buried as leaves began to fall.

Planted deep and covered up
Soil thrown in, pressed tight
Buried deep in darkness cold
Forgotten, out of sight.

The days of Winter passed
The snow, the wind, the rain
The gardener watched with longing
To see if life would come again.

She knew what lay inside the bulb
The beauty in the ground
She knew it only needed time
For that beauty to be found.

One day she saw a thin green shoot
Had pushed up to the light
She gently touched the fragile blade
And smiled with great delight.

And soon from out the darkness
Came a harbinger of Spring
A cheerful golden daffodil
Caused the gardener's heart to sing.

The Heavenly Gardener plants us
And waits for us to grow
He knows that in His perfect time
Flowers of faith and love will grow.

So wait with patience as He works
In the hidden, darkest place
For in His time, He will produce
The beauty of His Grace.

2019

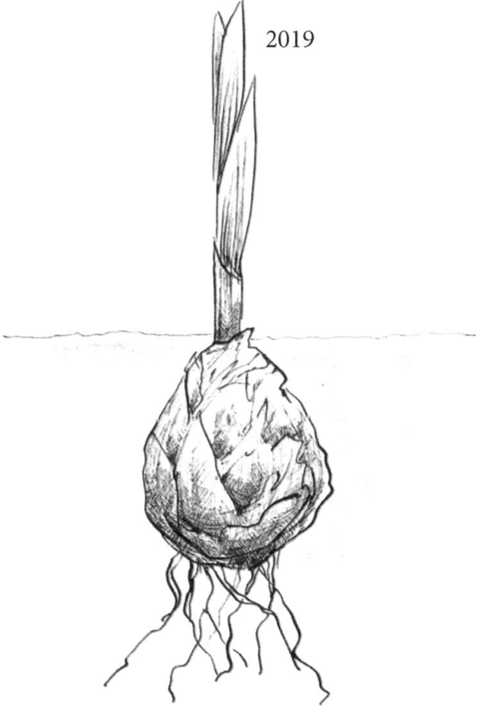

The following day was St Patrick's Day, affording the church a wonderful opportunity to engage with the community once again. Some folks braved the walk from Saul Church to Down Cathedral, the young people organised a float on the theme of 'The Greatest Showman', joining in with the parade with great enthusiasm, chocolate bars were handed out in the street and the church was used by the council as a control point for the police and ambulance service. The church was also open for toilet facilities and cuppas for folks who needed somewhere to rest and those of us who stayed there had lots of opportunities to chat with our visitors and answer questions about the Journey church.

Easter was celebrated in two ways - our first baptismal service on Easter Sunday and the Eggsplosion on Easter Monday. For weeks we had been filling little Easter eggs with sweets - thousands of them! Then on Easter Monday, they were scattered over a grassy area in the playing field nearby, some were shot up into the air and the hundreds of children who had gathered rushed to pick them all up. Mayhem ensued but everyone seemed to have fun!

For the past year, we had been desiring to see a change in Downpatrick and we caught a tiny glimpse of it that day. After all had been cleared up - face painting tables folded, inflatables deflated, chairs brought back to the church, Tucker was heading back to his home. He saw that a group of people had gathered on one of the estate greens, stopped to ask what was happening and discovered that some of the parents who had been at the eggsplosion had encouraged their children not to open all the eggs they had collected - most children had a big bag full - then when they got home, they replicated the eggsplosion for some of the families who hadn't been able to attend! Sharing the love! Changing Downpatrick little by little!

If we were honest, I think we would all have to admit to a need for change within us - a personal, deep desire to know God better, to draw closer to Jesus, to be more constantly filled with the Holy Spirit. The request of the two disciples on the road to Emmaus that He would 'stay' longer with them resonated with me when one of the speakers preached on it in the church:

ON THE ROAD TO EMMAUS

Jesus...
Won't You stay a little longer,
Linger here a little while?
Don't go on ahead without me,
Leaving me without Your smile.

Jesus...
What a joy to walk beside You
Listening to Your tender voice,
Speaking words of strength and comfort,
Words that made my heart rejoice.

Jesus...
As Your Presence filled completely
How my heart burned deep inside.
Stay a while, for I am longing
In that Presence to abide.

Jesus...
Now You've opened up my eyes,
Do not vanish from my sight.
Won't You stay a little longer,
Bathe my soul in God's pure light.

Jesus...
Stay a little longer
Come a little closer
Speak a little louder
Hold a little tighter
Touch a little deeper
Love a little stronger.

2019

That wee poem was written the day before our son, Marcus, married Alison - written, I think, on the ferry on the way to Scotland, where we enjoyed a beautiful ceremony and a fabulous meal in the pretty little town of Troon. While in Scotland, we took the opportunity to have a holiday in the area and I was able to fulfil a long-held ambition to visit the Isle of Iona. I have always been drawn to Celtic spirituality and church history and was so pleased to be able to walk around the tiny island where it is thought the amazing Book of Kells was copied.

IONA

The walk down the slipway to the ferry felt like the beginning of a pilgrimage. Just across the Sound of Mull, I could see the green outline of the island of Iona. Iona... I had heard of the Iona Community, I had read about Columba's journey to this tiny island in the sixth century so when the opportunity to visit the Inner Hebrides arose, the main focus of my planning was to see Iona. The interest in Celtic Christianity had begun many years earlier and had been developed by my use of the Celtic Daily Prayer readings and visits to our church from one of the members of the Northumbrian Community. So I understood the concept of pilgrimage and was looking forward to the prospect of walking where Columba and his monks had walked and worshipping and reflecting on the sacrifices they had made to bring the Gospel to Pagan people in Scotland.

I felt a measure of affinity with Columba - I came from Ireland... from Downpatrick where Patrick first landed when he carried the Gospel to Ireland and where both Patrick and Columba are buried under a huge granite stone in the graveyard of Down Cathedral. I too had travelled by sea to Scotland, albeit in a much more comfortable vessel than Columba's coracle! I had also been a missionary in a foreign land, and like Columba, I liked to write and sing.

Excitement grew as the ferry slowly forged a path through the blue waters of the Sound and gently deposited its travellers, mostly foot passengers, as cars are not permitted, on the slipway of Iona. The island, which lies off the south-west corner of Mull, is a long thin strip of land that looks as though some hungry giant had broken off a piece of a cookie. Its low buildings hug the shore, and some cows and sheep graze the fields beyond.

Our pilgrimage began with food - some sandwiches eaten on a bench looking out over the Sound. We had company - cheeky birds flew down, hoping to join in the feast - but apart from their fluttering and cheeping, there was no sound to distract us. I soaked up the quiet and thought that I would quite like to live in a place where only a few residents' vehicles are permitted - no noisy traffic, no smelly fumes.

We explored the ruins of the nunnery first - an addition much later than Columba's time - he brought only men to the island. Although in ruins, it was easy enough to trace the outlines of many of the rooms where women had shut themselves away to serve Christ by lives of prayer and poverty. Some volunteers from Scottish Heritage were doing restoration work and pointed out the stone seats where the nuns sat each day to confess their sins. I took one of the seats and wondered how it would have felt to sit on that cold stone seat and search my soul for ways I had displeased my God.

The road from the nunnery to the Abbey winds past an ancient Celtic cross, Maclean's cross. At the next corner, we paid a hurried visit to the old parish church and manse - the latter now serves as a heritage centre but the church is still a place of worship and I was intrigued to discover a beautiful wood carving of the Last Supper on the communion table. As time was limited, we quickly made our way to the Abbey, stopping only to read the information board outside the MacLeod Centre, which detailed the formation of the Iona Community in 1938 and the work of the centre which caters for families, youth groups and disabled visitors. The community and its volunteers have been responsible for some of the restoration work at the Abbey and also for keeping alive the centuries-old tradition of daily worship within its walls.

There is a sense of peace in the area surrounding the Abbey which even the many tourists seemed to feel, speaking quietly together as they walked through the ancient graveyard, where Scottish kings, including Duncan and Macbeth, are buried; admired the two high crosses near the Abbey door or read the placards at the well and Oran's Chapel. I was drawn to a rocky knoll which faces the entrance and discovered that it is thought to be the site of Columba's writing room - a simple wooden hut, no longer there, of course, where he spent long hours copying the Scriptures. I tried to imagine how disciplined he must have been to persevere at his task in all weathers and with only a candle to light the pages at night. And I remembered visiting the magnificent Book of Kells in Trinity College Dublin and being awestruck by the colours and the attention to detail - its other name is 'The Book of Columba' and tradition says that it was copied on Iona either by Columba or by some of the monks who followed him. How worthwhile were those hours spent in the writing room!

Inside the Abbey complex, visitors can wander through the cloisters, visit St Columba's Shrine - a tiny chapel beside the main door of the Abbey - see Columba's pillow stone with its engraved cross, learn that his strong singing voice could be heard on Mull as he worshipped, admire the stained glass windows or the marble altar but for me, the highlight of my visit was being able to participate in a short prayer service led by a member of the Iona Community. We made our way to the medieval choir stalls and along with others from countries across the world, listened to the readings, joined in the liturgy and the Lord's Prayer then spent a few moments in quiet personal prayer - a special privilege, indeed.

Soon afterwards we made our way back to the ferry and crossed the Sound of Mull but there was to be a postscript to our visit, one that would allow us to see the present island community working together wonderfully. We were about to set out on our way back to Tobermory when I realised that I had left my phone somewhere on the island. What were we to do? My resourceful, very friendly husband had got chatting to the owner of a craft shop we had visited and they had exchanged business cards so he phoned this lovely lady who encouraged us to return to the island and search for it. Meanwhile, she told us she would alert the island community by sending round an email. We hurried back on to the little ferry and were given a free ride when we explained why we were going back. We retraced our steps, telling our story to folks along the way. One of the Scottish Heritage workers insisted on helping our search by checking the area where we had eaten lunch but there was no phone to be seen anywhere. Not wishing to miss what we thought was the last ferry, we made our way back to the slipway. The very friendly husband was chatting to some of the Museum staff as we waited when a call came through from the craft shop owner to say that a phone had been handed into the hotel. When Robert expressed his dismay that there was no time to return there before the ferry set sail, one of the men he was chatting to informed him that there was a workers' ferry in half an hour.

So we both started running to the hotel, Robert out in front. Suddenly a van pulled up beside me and the Scottish Heritage worker asked if we had found the phone yet. I told him the story.

'Jump in, I'll bring you to the hotel', he said, 'and after you check if the phone is yours, wait at the hotel - I'll come back and bring you to the ferry.'

The phone was mine; the hotel receptionist was happy to give it to me when I demonstrated that I could unlock it, the van returned for us and we were in time to catch the very last ferry to Mull. I was struck by the response of our good Samaritan when we tried to thank him for his help -

'You know,' he said, 'it has just made my day that you were able to find your phone!'

The spirit of community is alive and well on the beautiful island of Iona!

It was easy to sense the presence of God in that quiet place and it reminded me once again that change in me could only come from spending time in His Presence as those early saints had done. When Crawford threw out a challenge to those who attended The Gathering some months later, to write the lyrics of a hymn and he would set it to music, I couldn't help but rise to the challenge! When I tried to think of a theme, my mind immediately jumped to what God had been developing within me - a desire for His Presence. Writing a hymn isn't as easy as writing a poem - the rhythms have to be tighter and it has to 'sing' well when put to music but Crawford and I were happy enough with the result and it was sung at the next meeting!

IN YOUR PRESENCE

There's a peace only found in Your Presence
Contentment only found at Your feet
So draw me, my Lord, to this place of rest
To stillness and fellowship sweet.

Chorus
In Your Presence... there is fullness of joy
In Your Presence... Your love is mine
In Your Presence... There I find perfect peace
In Your Presence... Your Presence divine.

There's a joy only found in Your Presence
Rejoicing in the midst of my tears
This joy is my strength, found in You alone
May joy rise and conquer my fears.

There's a love only found in Your Presence
Compassion that Jesus revealed
Come, fill me, my Lord with Your tenderness
To reach out and see others healed.

May I often be found in Your Presence
Abiding, welcomed there by Your Grace
So call me each day, by Your Love divine
To meet You, my Lord, face to face.

2019

One of the changes I want to see in my life is a greater awareness of His Presence so that even on an ordinary walk on a sunny October day, I will find my heart drawn to Him.

OCTOBER GIFT

This day was a gift
Unexpected in cold October
Wrapped in Autumn colours
Under a clear blue sky
The boardwalk firm beneath our feet
Carried us across the dunes
Hills of sand and pointy grass
Dressed in fern and heather.
The sea played peek -a- boo
Behind the waves of dunes
Until we reached the beach
And there it was in all its glory
The restless Irish Sea.
It should have been forbidding
Angry, stern and grey
On this October day
Instead, it wore a dress of blue
Its dancing waves a ruffle on the hem.
They sang a song to calm my soul
And cause my mind to ponder
The deep eternal mysteries
Of life and faith and God.
My gaze was drawn to nearby hills
Their soaring outline softest grey
In this early evening light
Sweeping down to meet the Irish Sea
Great mounds of granite rock

Clad in swathes of forest green
Solid, firm, immovable
Shouting out the Glory of my God.
This day was a gift
Wrapped in the song of dancing waves
My heart's response, a song
Of thankfulness.

2019

This year, 2020, began with a decision that grew out of a desire to see a change in me - our church runs a training course for those who have a similar desire or who want to develop tools that are useful to help others make changes. It's called 'Theotherapy' and, as suggested by the name, it combines theology and psychology. I'm finding it all very interesting if slightly brain-frying at times! I've been attending now for a few months and I suspect that God is going to use it to challenge me to desire change even more - watch this space!

CHAPTER 15

UNWELCOME CHANGE

We first heard about it in January - a new virus that had emerged in China - a coronavirus. We read the reports of the havoc it was creating in Wuhan - many people infected, many people dying, hospitals overwhelmed. But China was thousands of miles away and so life went on much as normal here in Northern Ireland. We celebrated my 70th birthday that month - a party for family and friends at Tami and Andy's house, followed by a few days at Portstewart. Our eldest granddaughter flew in from Australia to stay with us for six months, we began Equip 2020 modules in the church and we had our son's little dog Mo to stay with us now and again.

Then the first unwelcome change came in February - Tami phoned to say that she was on her way to the hospital with her eldest girl, Emma. The previous November Emma had suffered a pneumothorax (a collapsed lung) but had recovered quite well after being treated with oxygen. She was sent home but with a warning that it could happen again and that was why they were on their way to the hospital. That was the beginning of an almost three-week stay, that would culminate in surgery and a painful recovery. It was a stressful time for all concerned and I was so thankful that I had lots of friends in many churches who prayed for us through that difficult period.

Tami's other three girls stayed with us for most of that time, so it was a return to school runs and homework and cooking for a family of six. The girls were happy - a three-week sleepover at Nanna and Grandad's house was just brilliant for them and we enjoyed it too but could have done without the accompanying fatigue! The girls went back home on 6th March and Lysander's wee dog arrived to stay with us on 7th - he and Claire were off to Australia for three weeks and Mo came to stay with us. This was a different routine - a wee dog to walk and feed and waken us up in the morning - she was supposed to sleep downstairs but that didn't last long - she much preferred our bedroom!

Meanwhile, the tiny invisible enemy was making its destructive way across countries and continents and soon we heard the news of the first coronavirus case in the UK.

Other countries were shutting their borders and isolating the vulnerable and Lysander and Claire had to cut short their holiday, managing to catch one of the last flights out of Dubai on their way home. We prayed them the whole way home!

Lockdown began in the UK on 23rd March - an unwelcome change indeed. Two days later I posted a poem on Facebook, a friend asked if I would make it public so that she could share it and that was the start of the 'Lockdown poems' - once a week for the first ten weeks of lockdown.

This chapter will take on a different format from previous chapters - it will consist of the ten poems with a little explanation for each one. So settle down for a wee glimpse into what Lockdown was like for me!

I'm very aware that my experience of Lockdown has been much less traumatic than that of others - so far I have not succumbed to Covid-19, nor has anyone in my family and I have suffered no bereavement; I have not served, as many others have, on the frontline, caring for sick or dying patients, worrying about bringing the virus home; I have not lost my job or business; I have not been locked down in an abusive household. The sense of loss or inconvenience I have known, while real to me, has been trivial when compared to what others have endured. I do believe, however, that the poems written during Lockdown have a wider purpose than just to bring comfort or encouragement to me personally - my prayer is that many who had a very different experience to mine will be blessed by reading them.

LOCKDOWN POEM NO 1

In His Grip

The last Equip module I was able to attend before Lockdown was led by a friend I've known for a long time her husband Wes and our son Marcus played together for many years. Lynsey had been asked to lead a workshop on Prophetic Art and had it not been Lynsey leading it, I might not have gone, as I have no artistic talent at all. My brother Ray got all the artistic talent in our family! Seeing the paper and paints and pastels all laid out just confirmed for me that I was way outside my comfort zone, but I took a seat at one of the tables and waited.

Lynsey broke us in gently and the first exercise was fine - she had prayerfully completed some small pastel drawings before the module and simply invited us to go to the table and pick up whichever one we were drawn to - I could cope with that! My eye instantly lit upon a drawing of clasped arms and I picked it up... and I knew why I had picked it up. It reminded me of an illustration I have often used to reassure folks that even if we loosen our grip on God, His grip on us never loosens. As I turned the little drawing round and round, I found different facets of meaning - one way said that He lifts me when I'm down, another way said that He holds on to me when I try to escape and go my own way, another spoke of God's grasp as the comforting grasp of a friend but always, His grip was tighter than mine.

We were then asked to show it to the person beside us and explain what God had said through it, then invite that person to say what he saw in the picture.

I was sitting beside Thomas and his reply surprised me,

'I didn't see any of that at all - the moment I saw your picture, I thought it was a picture of you and how you support other people.'

That was, of course, a lovely encouragement to me in my one-to-one ministry into which God had led me in Journey.

I remembered that little picture when the virus came closer and closer to home and it was easy to find fear creeping in - what if I get the virus? What if I had to be put on a ventilator? What if someone in my family gets the virus? How would I cope with not being allowed to visit them? When my thoughts strayed in that direction, I would remind myself that God holds me in His grip and won't ever let go and two days after Lockdown began, I wrote the first poem.

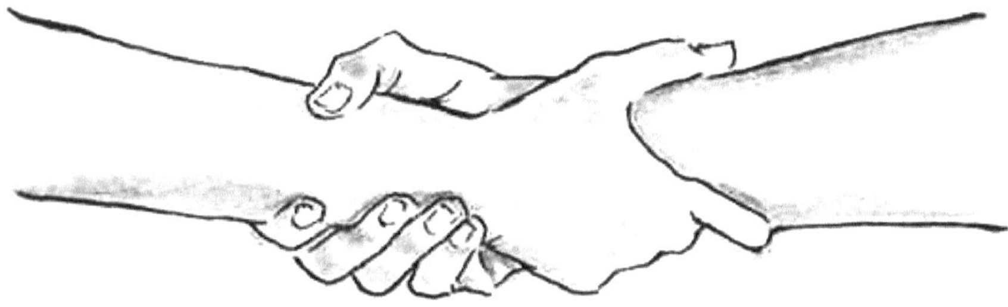

IN HIS GRIP

The nation waits
Breath held,
Stomach knotted,
Eyes fearful,
Under siege
Not at gunpoint
Not by armies
Nor by far-flung missiles
But by an unseen enemy.

The nation watches
As the enemy creeps on
Spreading
Invading
Relentless in its march
Ruthless in its reach
Circling the fragile earth
And then comes knocking at our door.

The nation weeps
As life is stripped
Of all but bare essentials,
No high fives, hugs or handshakes
No eating out or concert trips
Gifts are left on window sills
And church is on an iPad.
Then one by one the numbers rise
As loved ones fight for breath
And many lose the fight,
The nation joins in mourning.

What gives me peace
When fear is at my door?
What chases fear away?
Just this -
God holds me in His grip!
His strong, firm, loving grasp.
My hold may sometimes loosen
But His remains the same.
Held fast in life or death,
For now or for eternity,
In deep distress or greatest joy
His loving grip of Grace holds fast.
He'll never let me go.

When peace floods in
Fear has to flee...
My God has got a grip on me!

25th March 2020

LOCKDOWN POEM NO 2

Lockdown

By the second week, we were beginning to find that the novelty of Lockdown had worn off and the initial fear had dissipated (mostly!) but the inconvenience of it all had started to come to the fore. We had to learn to 'social distance', we couldn't shake hands with anyone, and we couldn't do our shopping because we were deemed to be elderly (much to our outrage). Fortunately our Granddaughter Ellie was allowed to shop for us - for essentials (yes, fudge is essential!) but there was no question it was inconvenient having to make lists instead of browsing the aisles. We couldn't visit our other granddaughters or attend church meetings - Facetime and Zoom and online streaming helped but it's not the same as meeting 'in the flesh'. We had lots of time on our hands, but we couldn't explore our beautiful island. We had wonderful weather, but we couldn't go to the beach - for me, the call of the sea is very strong so that was a great inconvenience - more than that, a loss!

I was grateful that the daily walk I was allowed meant that I could go to Saul Church, a lovely little church built on the site of Patrick's first church, a barn loaned to him by a local man named Dichu. I was delighted to find that its doors were open and often made my way there during the lockdown - only one person was permitted to enter at a time and I was careful not to touch anything while I was there but it was a real joy to stand in a quiet place of worship and pray or sing. Those who visited were encouraged to pray a prayer that had been attached to the front door - a prayer for Ireland, typed out in English and Irish - what a great idea! From its graveyard, I could just catch a glimpse of a tiny strip of blue in the distance - Strangford Lough - and that had to satisfy my longing for the sea during these strange weeks.

Then one morning I remembered the story of Noah and went back to Genesis to check the facts - yes, his lockdown had been as long as I thought - twelve and a half months, according to Genesis 8v13-14! That inspired poem no 2 - simply called Lockdown.

LOCKDOWN

I'm not too keen on lockdown
No big fan of staying in
Much rather get into my car
And go off for a spin!
I'd drive up to Portstewart
And walk along the strand
Listen to the waves roll in
Then sit on golden sand.
My eyes would feast on blue
The blue of sky and sea
The music of the lapping waves
Would soothe and comfort me.

But I am stuck in lockdown
Can't pop out to the shop
Someone else must browse the shelves
Leaving me to wield the mop!
Can't meet with other people
Just two who live with me
I'm missing all the friendly chats
With those I used to see.
It feels a bit like prison
Exercise just once a day
Orders that we have to keep
Visitors kept at bay!

But then I think of Noah
In lockdown on a boat
Eight people isolated
Hoping their ark would float.
Their situation worse than mine
In lockdown for a year!
I wonder were there moments
When their faith gave way to fear?
When everything they ever knew
Lay beneath the waters deep
Their homes, their friends, their way of life
Did they ever sit and weep?
They saw, when all was over,
And the rainbow curved above
That lockdown was salvation
An act of heavenly love.

So help me, God in Heaven
Not to rage or to complain
Not to see these days of lockdown
As nothing but a pain.
Help me see my isolation
As a gift from God above
An ark designed to keep me safe
An act of heavenly love.
So I will be content to rest
Live life a different way
Be grateful that in lockdown
I have time to read and pray
And may it draw me closer
To the One who is my King
May I see Him ever clearer
And my praises louder sing.

April 2020

LOCKDOWN POEM NO 3

THE KNOWING

Easter fell in the third week of Lockdown but all the usual Holy Week events were cancelled - no Easter conferences, no services bringing churches together to remember the Crucifixion on Good Friday, no dawn services to welcome Easter Sunday, no baptismal services, no family meals or outings, no Easter Monday eggsplosion. A very different Easter!

I spent some time meditating on the story of the anointing that had taken place in Bethany during the first Holy Week (found in John 12) and was impressed afresh with the realisation that, while Jesus often spoke to His disciples about His impending death, they didn't seem to take it in... but Mary did. Jesus rebuked the disciples' anger at her extravagance with these words:

'Leave her alone. She did this in preparation for my burial.'

My meditation led to poem no 3. There is just a subtle hint of Lockdown in the use of the word 'contagious' - a word often used in association with the nasty little virus that was sweeping through our land. What a challenge to think that my life could be 'contagious with the perfume of worship'.

THE KNOWING

She knew
What was to come
Heard Him speak of it often
Listened to the rumours
Murderous whispers
In the marketplace.

She paused
Outside the door
Knew that when she entered
She would face
That same hostility
A woman where she shouldn't be
Doing what she shouldn't do.

She grasped
The alabaster jar
Her eyes caressing
Its translucent beauty
A worthy keeper
Of the priceless nard within
Treasured and precious.

She entered
Hurried to His side
Ignored the collective gasp
Shattered the jar
Beauty broken into pieces
Poured the ointment on His feet
A sacrificial offering.

She knelt
In extravagant
Defiant worship
Released her hair
Her glory crown
In the shocked silence
Wiped His feet with her hair.

He knew
She saw it in His eyes
Heard it in His words
He knew her heart
Knew that she knew the truth
Of what would come
His life poured out.

He knew
This was no waste
No reckless loss
Of money or of reputation
She knew Him to be Lord
He saw her adoration
Worship poured out.

She carried
The sweet scent on her hair
She sang 'Hosanna!' with the crowd
Wept when she saw the cross
Rejoiced when He rose again
Spread all around the fragrance
Contagious with the perfume of worship.

I know
My life must be
Poured out for Him
A sacrificial offering
The fragrance of His Presence
Carried and shared
Contagious with the perfume of worship.

April 2020

LOCKDOWN POEM NO 4

He Lives

Easter Sunday morning has always been one of my favourite times in the church calendar. After the darkness and suffering of Good Friday and the sorrow of lost dreams and hopes on the second day, Sunday morning brings such joy. Resurrection hymns are triumphant and uplifting, listening to the story being read from Scripture, written by those who were there, is wonderful and most Easter Sunday sermons have just made my heart sing.

This year I was particularly drawn to the concept of power - the power of God that raised Jesus from the dead and in my next poem tried to imagine what it may have been like. It never ceases to amaze me that this same power is available to us today:

> *'I also pray that you will understand the incredible greatness of God's power for us who believe Him. This is the same mighty power that raised Christ from the dead and seated Him in the place of honour at God's right hand in the heavenly realms'.* (Ephesians 1:19-20 NLT)

HE LIVES!

A surge of power Divine
Penetrated tomb walls
The Father coming to His Son
His Son so well-beloved
The One who paid sin's price
Now cold and lifeless in the grave.
The Father touched the Son
A heart once still began to beat
Blood flowed once more in veins
Flesh flushed with life
A body broken regained strength
Wounds healed but not all disappeared
Nail prints in hands and feet
And wound in side remained
Proof for doubters of identity.
The power Divine flowed deeper
Touching molecules and cells
Reaching the minutest atom
Changing, transforming, glorifying.
The stone rolled back
The Son arose
And Light of world
Stepped into light of day
His body ready for eternity
Able to flow through earthly walls
Appear and disappear at will
And would in fifty days
Defy the law of gravity
To reach the Father's Throne.
What joys were waiting there?
Did angel voices sing His praise

Did harps and trumpets play
Did cherubim and seraphim
Bow low before the King
And did a cry go up, 'He lives!
And sin can be forgiven
The sons of men can come at last
To taste the joys of Heaven.'
And did the Son approach the Throne
To take His rightful place
So souls redeemed could stand there too
And see God face to face?

April 2020

LOCKDOWN POEM NO 5

Joy

I suppose it's hardly surprising that most of us know someone who succumbed to the coronavirus in 2020. It was disturbing to see the number of infections rise every day and to hear the reports of how difficult it was to treat those who had to be hospitalised. Our little Journey ladies' prayer group, the Olive Tree prayer group, were sent many requests for prayer and we were delighted to bring those requests to the Father's throne. We are grateful to God for answering those prayers.

One of our own members, Claire, became sick with suspected Covid-19 in March and I sent her a text asking if she was well enough for me to give her a ring. And so began a very special period of keeping in touch while she struggled with the roller coaster that is Covid-19. Some days there was good news - no cold sweats for a whole day, less lung pain or her voice becoming stronger but at other times she was 'wiped out' and couldn't even answer the phone. On one occasion, her voice completely disappeared and all I could do was just phone and pray over her.

I was chatting to her on the phone one day and she mentioned that the previous day had been a good day - she had been able to take a little walk outside. She remarked how beautiful everything looked in the sunshine, even the dandelions and her joy at seeing those dandelions inspired poem no 5.

JOY!

Joy isn't lost
In this shutdown place
Where we can't meet each other
Or chat face to face.

Joy isn't lost
It has not gone away
It isn't in hiding
Hasn't faded to grey.

Joy can be found
If you look all around
One glimpse of a flower
Or even a weed
And joy comes unbidden
As much as you need.

The bright dandelion
So greatly maligned
Is a sweet source of nectar
For bees, you will find.

And daisies are great
For children to pick
A bracelet, a necklace
Can be made in a tick.

Joy can be found
If you look all around
In life's simple things
God's hand can be seen
He paints with bright colours
And soft shades of green.

Pink blossoms of cherry
God's own work of art
A feast for my eyes
Giving joy to my heart.

And don't get me started
On beauty of roses
Soft petals to touch
And fragrance for noses.

Joy can be found
If you look all around
Find joy in creation
In flower or weed
Let joy come unbidden
As much as you need.

April 2020

When circumstances are difficult, we often find that there is still joy to be found, often in the simple pleasures of life.

The roller coaster continued for Claire with good days and bad days, until a point near the end of May when I received an urgent phone call from her,

'Gloria, I'm in the hospital, please pray!'

I have asked Claire to tell the story of God's miraculous intervention that day in her own words and I wish you could hear her lovely Cork accent as she tells it!

I was diagnosed as a suspected Covid-19 case on March 30th and was finding it hard to recover. I was just finishing a second

antibiotic when I woke up with severe pain in my left lung. Although I still had shortness of breath and general chest pain, this pain was different. It was 5.30 in the morning and I asked God what should I do. I heard a voice say, 'get dressed, pack a bag and go to hospital'. Being suspected Covid-19 I now faced a dilemma. I couldn't travel with anyone as that would put them at risk, I felt I wasn't sick enough to call an ambulance (when I was growing up you only called one if your leg was hanging off or you were almost dead!) so that left one remaining option. I would drive myself to the hospital - the nightmare being my closest hospital was a 45-minute drive away.

I rested for a few hours to try and get the strength I'd need to drive and I felt the peace of God take away any worry. At 10 o'clock I called my friend Gillian who just happened to be expecting a call from me. I believe God did that. He put me on her mind and it was no surprise to her that I'd need her help. How good is God? She would drive in front of me and if I felt I needed to stop for a rest on the journey to the hospital we had a signal system. I would flash my lights and beep the horn.

At this stage, every breath hurt. I'm a stubborn Cork woman and I was determined to drive all the way no matter what. However about halfway through the journey, I felt incredibly weak and knew I wasn't safe to continue without a break. Going through a village I saw the perfect place to pull in so flashed the lights, blasted the horn but Gillian never heard or saw me and she kept on driving. Panic set in. I caught up with her, flashed the lights again and she pulled in but it was a section of the road that wasn't safe. Gillian then remembered a football pitch close by. It would be closed due to lockdown so it would be safe for me to get out of the car and rest.

Sure enough, the place was empty. Even getting out of the car was an effort and I just wanted to lie down. As I tried to control my breathing, a car entered the grounds. O no! I prayed, 'Please God let them understand and not move us on.' The man just happened to be there at that time as he needed to do a bit of maintenance and when Gillian explained what was happening, he was happy to leave us be. After a few minutes, another car arrived. What now!! Gillian got ready to explain things again but before she needed to even utter a word, the lady stepped out of her car and said she worked with Covid-19 patients. She explained that her husband, the man doing the maintenance, had rung her; that she should be at her workplace but just happened to be working from home for the first time in days instead. Gillian and I just looked at each other with eyes wide and said 'God.' This was a miracle. If we had pulled in when I first flashed the lights, this would not have happened.

The lady was able to assess me and call an ambulance. She also advocated on my behalf with the paramedics, as my vital stats were good but my colour and breathing were abnormal and the pain was almost unbearable. I was transported to hospital by ambulance and the horrendous pain was explained by blood test results - a blood clot. This was just beginning to be recognised by the doctors as a possible side effect of Covid-19. I couldn't believe it... there is no history of blood clots in my family and then the seriousness of this hit me. What if the clot had moved when I was driving, what if I had caused an accident? God stepped in to protect, not just me, but other road users. Once I heard it was a blood clot, I quickly rang Gloria and Sharon, to ask church members to pray. Also, I contacted close family and friends to ask them to pray. The peace of God was continuous. I knew I was in His hands. I got an injection of heparin and was sent for a CT Scan. The doctor returned with the results looking stunned. Praise God another miracle, no sign of the blood clot!!

God, who looks after the flowers of the fields and clothes them more beautifully than Solomon, cares oh so much more for me. He sees us, He tenderly loves us and He is a miracle-working God. All glory to God.

LOCKDOWN POEM NO 6

CURLED UP WITH A BOOK

As the weeks went by, it was remarkable just how inventive and creative people had to become to maintain connection. Churches moved either to pre-recorded services or to live-streamed services - sometimes a mixture of both. The Journey church in Antrim turned the main room in their Antrim offices into a recording studio and managed to deliver live services while maintaining social distancing, of course! Mid-week meetings used the Zoom platform so that we could see each other and interact. The counselling course I'm doing was held via Zoom, as were Mission Africa council meetings and even the mission's Summer conference. On one memorable occasion I was on Zoom from 10 am to 1 pm, from 2 pm until 5 pm and from 7:30 until 9 pm - I was in bed by 9:30! Zoom was very tiring!

The Olive Tree prayer group kept in touch via Facebook messenger but the ladies I pray with on Fridays had a slightly more complex arrangement. As Pat doesn't use a smartphone, we began by connecting the other three of us by WhatsApp, then I used Robert's phone to contact Pat and put her on speaker so that we could all hear each other. Unfortunately, the speaker on my phone wasn't working too well and I had to tilt the phone to speak into the bottom of it and so Gwen and Lavinia ended up talking to the ceiling! We then decided to use Zoom instead and that worked better but it was still quite a complicated process! We did manage one socially distanced visit to Pat's garden as the lockdown began to ease but those types of meetings were weather dependant and didn't always work.

The Writers' Group I attend solved the problem in another way - we became an online group - prompts were sent out by email once a month and our responses were emailed back to our secretary, Heather, who then collated them and sent copies to everyone. It worked very well, and it was great to receive all the poems and short prose pieces that others had written. I sent in this wee poem as my response to the prompt 'Curled up with a book' and then brought a copy over to the granddaughters, standing at the front door to read the poem that mentioned their Mum.

CURLED UP WITH A BOOK

In my earliest days
When Mum came to look
I'd be under the blankets
Curled up with a book.

When I later got married
And time came to cook
My husband would find me
Curled up with a book.

My daughter was fed
In my favourite nook
Held closely for comfort
Curled up with a book.

So it's not a surprise
It wasn't a fluke
She can often be found
Curled up with a book.

So each in her armchair
By hook or by crook
We'll conquer this virus
Curled up with a book.

Where might you find us
If an earthquake shook?
We'd be under a table
Curled up with a book!

May 2020

LOCKDOWN POEM NO 7

God's Whisper

It was a chilly evening in May, so we lit the fire. There was no one else in the room so I raised the footrest of the recliner settee and toasted my toes while I settled down to engage with the Friday evening Praise and Prayer sessions run by the church. The praise led by Joshua and Marah was quietly worshipful and in one of the breaks, Richard Porter (the Pastor Emeritus) told the story of Elijah's encounter with the 'gentle whisper' of God on Mount Sinai. He encouraged us to enter the Presence of God and there listen for His still small voice. There was a real sense that evening that the Presence of God was filling the room where they were worshipping but also of that same Presence filling the room where I was sitting. How amazing is our God? When I woke up the next morning, the lines of this little poem began to form and it became poem no 7. One way to find peace in life's changing and difficult circumstances is to enter His Presence and rest there a while.

GOD'S WHISPER

Come away for a while
Come and rest at My feet
Enter into My Presence
Its fragrance so sweet.

Hush, My beloved
Just rest and be still
My Spirit comes gently
Your heart He will fill.

Lay aside all your worries
Your stresses and fear
Give yourself to My Presence
And I will draw near.

My whispers are heard
In a quiet heart
In stillness and silence
When I call you apart.

This poem is a whisper
I heard in my ear
My heart was at rest
And the Father drew near.

So I'm giving it back
As an offering of love
In response to His whisper
From Heaven above.

May 2020

LOCKDOWN POEM NO 8

BROKEN STUMP

When we moved to our new little house in the summer of 2018, one of the first jobs we tackled was the tiny garden at the back. The fence on one side was completely overgrown by a rather rampant climber - we didn't even know what type of plant it was, but we decided that it had to go! So the loppers came out and it was attacked with great enthusiasm. As we proceeded, we uncovered a lovely little stone wall and a flower bed behind it. Now all that was needed was to get rid of the two roots that had been feeding the climber - easier said than done! Robert tried the axe and the saw, dug down beside them to try and prise them loose but all to no avail and we were left with two stubborn roots that just would not be shifted.

Through the next year, every time shoots appeared from those roots, they were dealt with mercilessly. The following year we decided to allow the shoots to grow but watched them carefully and trimmed them back when required. To our amazement, beautiful little flowers appeared on one of the climbers and we realised that the invader was a rather gorgeous clematis that bloomed in May during the lockdown.

When John Ashe spoke on Revival and reminded us how often in the past revival had come at times when the Church was at a particularly low ebb, I was reminded of the broken stump in our garden and wrote poem number 9 - a cry from the heart that the Holy Spirit would spark a flame of revival even amid the devastation and heartbreak caused by the coronavirus. There were tiny indications that God was on the move - many thousands of people (1 in 4 according to reports) in the UK were tuning in to online services, others were googling 'prayer' and the We Serve team, set up by the Journey church to serve the community during the crisis, were finding a great openness in those they contacted and a willingness to accept the prayer that was offered by the volunteers. The enemy may have tried to use the virus for evil, but God was able to use it for good.

BROKEN STUMP

The gardeners tried to kill it
It had spread out far and wide
Climbed over posts and fences
Covered plants until they died.
So they pulled it
they broke it
they hacked it
they sawed it
Tried to dig the root up
But it would not be shifted
So they cut it down
And only a stump was left
'Victory!' they cried, 'It's dead!'

But in the Spring that followed
Life flowed up from the root
And from the stump once left for dead
Appeared a tiny shoot.
Nourished by food from root below
Watered by gentle rain.
First, it sent a feeler out
Then began to climb again.

It pushed
it clung
it budded
it grew
Then found a resting place.
Along the top of the fence it spread
Grew fast in the Summer heat
Blossomed and bloomed from the broken stump
That refused to admit defeat.

The enemy tried to kill it
It had spread out far and wide
Encroaching on his kingdom
A thorn in Satan's side.
He deceived it
he beat it
he stoned it
he sawed it
Tried to dig its root up
But the root would not be shifted
So he cut it down
Till only a stump was left
'The church is dead!' He cried.

But every time his victory cry
Rang out across the skies
The Root pushed out another shoot
And the Church began to rise
Nourished by food from Root below
Watered by Spirit's rain
Revival seeds burst forth once more
From worshipping hearts again.
The Spirit's fruit began to grow
Blooms of peace and joy and love
Repentant hearts came to the Cross
Mercy fell from Heaven above.

When the enemy shouts, 'I've won!'
And the Church seems to have died
Be sure that deep in the ruined stump
A shoot is hidden inside.
Listen then for another shout
To echo across the skies
'My Church is not defeated
It is ready to arise!'

Oh Holy Spirit, light a flame
Our passion to ignite
Let's fan that flame He sparks within
Set the world ablaze with Light!

May 2020

LOCKDOWN POEM NO 9

Behind the Wire

During lockdown Tami was homeschooling her four girls and encouraged the eldest, Emma, to pursue her interest in photography by taking an online course. She and Willow went off together one day and set up a photo of Willow inside a roll of wire that they found outside their house. They are both on the autistic spectrum and the younger one sent me her interpretation of the photo the next day:

'It represents people that have autism and how they can sometimes feel uncomfortable and it is not very easy to get past this hard time and they feel like they are locked in. (Just like me)'

I was thinking about the picture the next day and recalling the years I spent supporting and teaching pupils who were autistic - they were the best years of my teaching career. I enjoyed getting to know each one, trying to understand their unique way of seeing the world, discovering their strengths - their 'superpowers' and encouraging them to achieve their potential. Life was a struggle for most of them and I felt that Emma and Willow's photograph was a great visual representation of that struggle. I wrote the poem below with autism in mind but was aware that the 'wire' could stand for many other struggles in life, including lockdown.

BEHIND THE WIRE

I never fitted in
Always felt left out
So tears would fall
Behind the wire

A heart too tender
A skin too thin
Felt pain too keenly
Behind the wire

I heard their words
I saw them laugh
But jokes fell flat
Behind the wire

I prayed at night
When lockdown came
That people would be brave
Behind their wire.

For I could understand
The fear they felt
Fear of the unknown
Behind this wire

Others looking in
See the way I've grown
See my superpowers
Behind my wire

Someday I'll tell the world
What I have learnt
Share special gifts
Behind my wire

My tender heart
Will comfort those
Who also find themselves
Behind the wire

Till then, I'll search
For spaces here and there
Bravely reaching out
Beyond my wire

So if you see my hand
Hold it tenderly
Become my friend
Across the wire

May 2020

Writing 'Behind the Wire' reminded me of a poem I had written at the beginning of the year in response to another Writers' Group prompt - forgetfulness. It was about other people who live 'behind the wire' - those who live with dementia. Some of my friends have become carers for their spouses when they developed dementia, so I have learnt a little about the accompanying difficulties through listening to them.

THE SENSE OF ME

I've lost the sense of me
Who I am and who I used to be.
Myself just faded slowly, day by day
Absorbed into the mists of memory lost,
And now it's just a wraith
That can't be grasped or held.

You say you are my daughter...
But shouldn't there be a memory
Of silken skin or baby smell
Or sleepy, milky smile?
Sometimes deep within that hazy mist
A ghostly shape takes form -
A glimpse of beach, the roar of wave
A child runs screaming to the sea...
I search for words to share the fleeting glimpse
But words just melt into the tears
You see and try to wipe away...
'Please don't be sad,' you say
But I'm not sad -
Those tears are momentary joy
Mixed with a deep frustration.

One day some singers came
And sang the songs I used to sing
I joined in - singing all the words,
Words locked inside the music
Held there by rhythm and the melody.
For those brief moments, I was me again
Found by the joy that music brings.

So Daughter, can you sing to me?
And maybe I'll join in
Perhaps within the song, we'll reconnect
I'll know just who you are, as you know me
And maybe as I look into your eyes and sing
I'll find the sense of me I've lost
The sense of self I'm searching for in vain.
So sing, my lovely girl, come, sing to me.

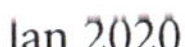
Jan 2020

Willow contacted me one evening via FaceTime and after a few moments she excused herself saying, 'I'm going now... I've got to pray.'

She was back quite quickly and told me she had prayed that people 'would be brave at this hard time' - I thought that was lovely! Maybe we should all pray that those 'behind the wire' would be brave in the midst of their struggle.

LOCKDOWN POEM NO 10

Oh Joy, Oh Joy, Oh Joy

By the end of May, the Lockdown restrictions were beginning to be lifted and one of the first places I visited was Ballyhornan - I just wanted to see the sea again! The excitement I felt when we drove through the little village and caught our first glimpse of the sea reminded me of childhood Sunday School excursions to either Newcastle or Portstewart. A big bus was hired as few families owned cars, a hall was booked in case it rained, sandwiches and cakes were made and off we went. We usually only visited the seaside twice a year and the first occasion was the excursion - the other was our annual holiday in July - so I felt the mounting excitement as the bus approached our destination. There was a point on the trip to Portstewart where the first glimpse of the blue sea could be caught - just at the top of the town, looking down towards the harbour - and it always filled me with joy! I felt that same joy when I saw the blue of the sea at Ballyhornan that day, then walked down on to the beach for the first time in months. I hope my last Lockdown poem expresses that joy.

OH JOY, OH JOY, OH JOY!

Oh joy, oh joy, oh joy!
The song played
Over and over in my head
As once again my eyes
Saw blue sky kiss blue sea
And joy rose up inside of me.
How I have missed the sea
So every sense was heightened
Smelt the tangy sea smell
Felt soft sand yield to my feet
Touched its warmth with my palm
Rested my fingers in its silky smoothness
Heard the rhythm of its music
Soothe and quieten my soul within
Till breathing slowed and peace flowed in
Oh joy, oh joy, oh joy!

Smiled as unfurling waves
Chased seaweed up the beach
And hungry seagulls divebombed fish
Admired the long, thin island
Rising green and lovely close to shore
Watched a rowing boat moored there
Shift idly in the gentle breeze
Laughed as a tiny girl
Danced in the lapping waves
Then squealed at their icy touch
Loved how the dogs chased balls
And splashed along the water's edge
Their joy in freedom echoed mine
In sea and sand and warm sunshine
Oh joy, oh joy, oh joy!

May 2020

Further easing of restrictions brought more joy - socially distanced walks with the ladies from the Olive Tree prayer group, family birthday celebrations, hugs for the granddaughters (I think I may have gone a little early with this one but a lovely six year old surely needs a birthday hug and you couldn't possibly hug one granddaughter and not hug the other three, could you?) I was so looking forward to the time when we could meet up freely when we could shake hands and hug each other - air hugs didn't quite cut it! And I found it hard to wait until we would be able to meet in our lovely little Journey Community Church and worship together. I was in contact with quite a few folks from the Journey family during this period and repeatedly I heard the same phrases: 'I miss going to church... I miss singing together... I miss the connection... I miss the cups of tea and the chats...' Lockdown certainly emphasised just how much we need each other - we are designed to be in fellowship!

CHAPTER 16
A CHANGED WORLD

If going into Lockdown was hard, coming out was even harder. We emerged from the safety of our homes to find that the world had changed almost beyond recognition. No longer could we just 'pop up' to the shop - we had to remember our masks (which then steamed up our glasses so that we couldn't see what we were shopping for) we had to wait (sometimes outside the shop) two metres apart, we had to sanitise our hands and usually follow a one-way system and pay (preferably by card) the cashiers who worked behind perspex screens.

No longer could we make an impulsive decision to visit the National Trust properties nearby - we often used to wait for dry weather and then just go for a walk or a picnic on the spur of the moment but in this 'new normal', visits had to be booked, in some cases by the previous day. When Tami and Andy arranged a family holiday in August and invited us to join them, having to book visits presented one or two problems - weather apps had to be consulted to choose the best day to visit the Giant's Causeway and once a day and allotted time were chosen, we had to go, even though it started to rain on the way there. There was no bus to take us down the long road to the famous stones or, more importantly, bring us back up again! Because we had booked a session of mini golf on another day, we had to play in the pouring rain, and I can testify to how difficult it is to play while trying to hold up a big umbrella! Despite these setbacks, we still managed to have fun and make wonderful memories on both occasions!

When we were able to meet in church again, it was a different experience from pre-lockdown services - masks again, our temperature was taken at the door, sanitiser again, in the front door and out the back door, socially distanced seating, no Journey Kids, no touching in prayer ministry. But how good it was to be worshipping with other people again - a smaller number than usual but still, so good!

One of the greatest challenges in this changing world was having to make choices constantly - do we go to the church service and risk being in contact with someone who could infect us with Covid-19 or do we stay at home and watch it online? Do we risk eating out in a restaurant or stick to takeaways? Should we meet up with others or was it better to be careful? Was it wise to book flights or ferries and run the risk of having them cancelled and then face the hassle of claiming money back? The frequent changing of government advice just added to the confusion and the challenge. I felt sorry for those who faced much tougher questions - should I agree to go back to work even if I don't feel safe? Should I try to keep my business running even though it's not financially viable? How can I be sure that schools or universities will be safe places for my children?

What a blessing it was to believe that our God knew the answers to the questions we had and could help us to make the right choices!

THE CHALLENGE OF CHOICE

Lockdown was hard
But its message was clear
The virus is deadly
Don't let it come near.
Stay inside your home
Let no one come in
Keep washing your hands
Tissues go in the bin.
Cough into your elbow
Just one walk each day
Keep two metres distance
Keep the virus at bay.

We emerged at last from Lockdown
Stepping warily outside
Like bears who ventured out from dens
Sniffed the air, crept back to hide.

It all still felt too dangerous
The world was a different place
Longing to see the friends we'd missed
Scared to meet them face to face.

No message clear to guide us
Choices to make instead
Weighing up the risks we'd take
As we tried to plan ahead.

Go back to work or stay at home?
Travel abroad this year?
Go back to church or stay online?
Be brave or live in fear?

Help us make good choices, Lord,
When these challenges arise
You said we only have to ask
And You would make us wise.

We all need to remember
That You hold us in Your hand
That Your plan for us is perfect
Though we may not understand.

For Lockdown didn't shock You
Didn't take You by surprise
You know about the virus
When it lives and when it dies.

So I'll entrust my life to You
Rest in Your love for me
Know every day, in every way
Your goodness I will see.

August 2020

Life continued to be unpredictable and uncertain. Our Journey Church had opened for in-person services, then had to revert to live-streaming for a couple of weeks before opening up again. Fundraising events were planned and then had to be cancelled and the money raised another way. Our 'Toy Tales' effort, which raises money to help families who are struggling to buy presents for their children at Christmas, was affected by a mountain hike being cancelled twice! But we all learnt to be patient and to adapt to our changed world.

In the midst of all this change, God reminded me in a beautiful way that His love never changes - it never fails. Two of our grandchildren, Charlotte and Willow, came with us to one of the in-person services and were standing beside me for the worship. Each, in turn, came over to me as we were singing, for a 'Nanna huggle'. There was a very special sense of the Presence of God during the worship that morning - moments when God felt very near and very real. When I thought about those moments during the days that followed, this wee poem took shape.

DEEP LOVE, DEEP WORSHIP

She stepped into my worship
This daughter of my daughter
Encircling my waist
To hold me in a firm embrace
Of love.
We moved together
in a gentle dance
And sang of how God loves us.
She loves me
And I love her
And I love God
And she loves God
And God loves her
And God loves me.
He wrapped us round
With Love Divine.
As she could feel my heartbeat,
I felt His.
A moment of deep love.

He stepped into our worship
Third Person of the Trinity
To wrap us in the warm embrace
Of Divine Presence.
The Spirit stirred,
Our voices rose
A great crescendo
Of praise and exaltation
To the God of Heaven.
We sang for joy of Him
We sang in awe of Him
Our arms outstretched
Our hearts bowed low.
A moment of deep worship.

Two moments
Deep love
Deep worship.
Foretaste of Heaven -
Every moment
Deep love
Deep worship.

September 2020

CHAPTER 17

UNCHANGING GOD

The last five years of my life have been marked by change - so have I found peace in changing circumstances? Although I haven't found some of the changes particularly pleasant and wouldn't have asked for some of the changes that came my way, I can honestly say that I have found the *'Peace Whatever'* mentioned in Chapter 2. There is a peace that transcends circumstances, a peace promised by none other than Jesus Himself:

> *'I am leaving you with a gift - peace of mind and heart. And the peace I give is a gift the world cannot give. So don't be troubled or afraid.'* John 14:27 (NLT)

So how is this peace to be found? I think it is rooted in the truth that the God in whom I trust never changes. From the moment that I knelt at my bedside as an eleven-year-old girl and entrusted my life and future to Him, He has never changed. I have proved Him to be a faithful God. In fact, from the moment that He spoke, and the universe came into being, He has never changed. So my deep-rooted sense of security rests on the knowledge that God is the Unchanging One, that He is a good God and that He will always love me and watch over me.

So where is this peace to be found? Many times in the past 5 years, I have found my peace in His Word.

When He called me to wait, His Word assured me that those who wait on the Lord 'renew their strength.'

When change was difficult, Psalm 23 reminded me that He planned to *'restore my soul.'*

When conflict came, His Word said, 'forgive one another.'

When I remembered my failings, Jude's promise was that one day I would be 'presented faultless before the presence of His glory with exceeding joy.'

When I needed guidance about changing church, I read what Jesus said in Mark 2: '*New wine calls for new wineskins.*'

When I had doubts about the decision I had made, Psalm 16 gave me reassurance: '*I know the Lord is always with me, I will not be shaken, for He is right beside me.*'

When coronavirus swept through our world, I took comfort from the words of Psalm 18: '*The Lord is my rock, my fortress and my saviour, my God is my rock, in whom I find protection. He is my shield, the power that saves me and my place of safety.*'

When fear came knocking at my door, Psalm 63 spoke into my heart to remind me that '*Your strong right-hand holds me securely.*'

When Lockdown took away some of the joy in life, I remembered another verse from Psalm 16: '*In Your Presence, there is fullness of joy; at Your right hand are pleasures forevermore.*'

So when is this peace to be found? I think my answer to that question would be - when I surrender to the work of the Holy Spirit in my life. Part of the fruit of God's indwelling Spirit is peace:

'The Holy Spirit produces this kind of fruit in our lives: love, joy, peace, patience, kindness, goodness, faithfulness, gentleness and self-control.'

How wonderful to know that however the circumstances of our lives may change, we have an unchanging God and that in those circumstances, we can find the peace promised to us by Jesus, a peace that grows and develops within us as we yield to the presence of His Holy Spirit in our lives.

THE QUAKE OF CHANGE

The quake of change
May strike suddenly
Fiercely, violently
Tectonic plates of life
Shifting, grinding
Pushing up high mountain ranges
Of fear, anxiety and pain
Ripping my world apart.

The quake of change
May creep slowly
Subtly, silently
Tremors hidden deep
Rippling, shaking
Cracking a life well ordered
Spilling worry out, or doubt
Tearing my world apart.

Where do I run
When hit by quake of change?
Where is my solid ground?
Where can my peace be found?

I'll run to God
The Great Unchanging One
The One who is my rock
Strong, solid, immovable
The One who is my strength
Who holds me in His grip
He will be my fortress
My place of safety in the quake

High, mighty walls surround me
Eternal walls that never fall
He will be my shield
Arrows of change may fly
But never penetrate
Never pierce my heart
Never thwart His purposes.

Life may change
God stays the same
I'll run to Him
Call out His Name
My life is safe
I need not fear
When changes come
My God draws near
The quake can't touch
What God holds tight
So I'm at peace
By day, by night
Let changes come
My God above
Will hold me still
Within His love.

Thousands of years ago, when God instructed Moses to tell Aaron how to bless the people of Israel, these beautiful words were recorded for us in Numbers 6.

'The Lord bless you and keep you; the Lord make His face to shine upon you and be gracious unto you; the Lord turn His face toward you and give you peace.'

In the days of Lockdown, many of us were blessed by various musical renditions of the Aaronic Blessing, recorded on the Zoom platform - people from many nations singing those ancient words of God over their countries. Our God hasn't changed - His heart has always been to bless His people, to be gracious unto them and to give them peace.

As I read more about this blessing, I discovered that the Ancient Hebrew Research Centre had examined it for its original Hebraic meaning and I particularly loved the way the Centre translated it:

'Yahweh will kneel before you presenting gifts and will guard you with a hedge of protection, Yahweh will illuminate the wholeness of His being towards you bringing order and He will beautify you, Yahweh will lift His wholeness of being and look upon you and He will set in place all you need to be whole and complete.'

May that be our experience in all the changing circumstances of our lives and may we all truly know the rich blessing of God who, by His Spirit, gives us His peace.

Other books by Gloria Kearney:

Sing in the Shadow	1999
Special Moments	2000
A Place Prepared	2002
Sunrise to Sunset	2005
The Voice in the Laburnum Tree	2007
A Sparrow's Tale (with Lavinia Abrol)	2009
Kingdom Park	2010
Songs from a Quiet Heart	2014

For more information about
AMBASSADOR INTERNATIONAL
please visit:
www.ambassador-international.com
@AmbassadorIntl
www.facebook.com/AmbassadorIntl

BV - #0001 - 021220 - C14 - 215/143/10 - PB - 9781649601919